CARDINALS
ESSENTIAL

Everything You Need to Know to Be a Real Fan!

David Claerbaut

TRIUMPH
BOOKS
CHICAGO

Library of Congress Cataloging-in-Publication Data

Claerbaut, David.
    Cardinals essential : everything you need to know to be a real fan / David Claerbaut.
      p. cm.
    ISBN-13: 978-1-57243-833-0
    ISBN-10: 1-57243-833-9
    1. St. Louis Cardinals (Baseball team)—Miscellanea.

GV875.S74C53 2006
796.357'640977866—dc22

2005055905

This book is available in quantity at special discounts for your group or organization. For further information, contact:

Triumph Books
542 South Dearborn Street
Suite 750
Chicago, Illinois 60605
(312) 939-3330
Fax (312) 663-3557

Printed in U.S.A.
ISBN-13: 978-1-57243-833-0
ISBN-10: 1-57243-833-9
Design by Patricia Frey
All photos courtesy of AP/Wide World Photos

To all those Cardinals fans out there,
this book is for you.

A Great Franchise

One way you can identify great sports franchises is by how little their logos change over the years, and few have changed as little as that of the St. Louis Cardinals. The *S*, *T*, and *L* overlaying one another is unmistakably St. Louis, and it is hard not to fall in love with that beautiful jersey logo, which, depending on the era, has one or two redbirds perched atop a yellow bat with the word *Cardinals* written in red script below.

Pittsburgh is a football town, Detroit a hockey city, and Indianapolis a basketball center. St. Louis, however, is a baseball town. More than that, it is a *Cardinals* baseball town. Hot weather, cold beer, and Cardinals baseball are nearly the definition of summer in St. Louis. KMOX, the Clear Channel radio station that broadcasts the Cardinals games, once ran a full-page ad in *The Sporting News*, the national, largely baseball sportsweekly published in St. Louis, at the outset of an upcoming baseball season. Beneath the call letters of the station, the ad contained but three words: *Baseball Spoken Here.*

Cardinals baseball is the native tongue of this Gateway to the West city. Not baseball, Cardinals baseball. Unlike the Braves, the Dodgers, the Giants, the Athletics, and others, the Cardinals are forever linked with just that one city—St. Louis—and St. Louis is forever linked to the baseball Cardinals. In fact, despite the existence of the NFL franchise with the same nickname, for most sports fans, the word *Cardinals* is as bonded to St. Louis as *Yankees* is to New York, *Red Sox* is to Boston, and *Cubs* is to Chicago.

And for good reason. The St. Louis Cardinals are the definition of stability. They have been called the Cardinals since 1900, been in St. Louis since 1882, and have called but three parks home for more than a century, through 2005. The NBA has come and gone from the city of the blues. The NFL is on its second team there, while the NHL planted an expansion franchise in the city of the Ozarks. But the Cardinals live on.

They also exude success. No National League team has won more World Series championships than the St. Louis Cardinals—not the Dodgers, not the Giants, not the Braves. In fact, if you include divisional and league championships, the Cardinals have posted 33 championships in their history. From the Gashouse Gang, to the Musial saga, to the Brock-Gibson championship years, to Whitey Ball, to the power teams of the new millennium, Cardinals history is one of great era after great era.

In fact, beginning in the twenties, the team has had only two decades—the seventies and the nineties—when it did not post a winning record for the 10-year period. And in each of those decades, the Redbirds were .500 or better in at least five of the ten years. And the current era is better than ever. In the first half of the Y2K decade, the Redbirds registered six straight winning seasons, averaging almost 96 wins a season from 2000 through 2005, including two 100-win seasons.

Great names dot the team's history. Rogers Hornsby, Frankie Frisch, Dizzy Dean, Joe Medwick, Enos "Country" Slaughter, Stan "the Man" Musial, Lou Brock, Bob Gibson, Ozzie Smith, and Albert Pujols are but 10 on-the-field examples of Cardinals greatness over the decades. Billy Southworth, Frisch, Red Schoendienst, Whitey Herzog, and Tony La Russa are managers who have patrolled the Cardinals dugout, while off-the-field legends like Branch Rickey, August "Gussie" Busch, Bob Broeg, Harry Caray, and Jack Buck are also part of Cardinals baseball lore.

"From the first time I put on a St. Louis Cardinals uniform," said the greatest Cardinal of them all, Stan Musial, "I knew I was part of something special." Musial, who first wore Cardinal Red in 1941, has never let go of the near-magical spirit associated with being a St. Louis Cardinal. "It was the feeling that Red Schoendienst and Enos Slaughter experienced—and why they became so upset and emotional when they

By the NUMBERS

106—Number of Cardinals wins in 1942, the most ever by a Cardinals team in a single season.

The 1926 Cardinals, managed by player/manager Rogers Hornsby, brought St. Louis its first World Series title.

were traded," the Man remarked. "Lou Brock and Bob Gibson had it, and so did Ozzie Smith and Mark McGwire. There have been so many great players on the Cardinals over the years, and each and every one of them knew how blessed they were."

Indeed, when you see Cardinals baseball in your mind's eye, you see Dizzy Dean or Bob Gibson firing a fastball, Lou Brock swiping second, Enos Slaughter rounding third, Curt Flood chasing down a rocket in center, or the Wizard of Oz turning a certain hit into a twin killing, and Stan the Man, Mark McGwire, or Albert Pujols ripping homers into the warm St. Louis night. And you see it all on the radio through the voices of Harry Caray and Jack Buck.

"St. Louis is a special town," said Musial, "and the fans of the Cardinals are something special." And those fans are as much a part of

TRIVIA

Which three men have managed the Cardinals for part or all of at least 10 seasons?

Answers to the trivia questions are on pages 161–162.

the Cardinals' identity as the players who proudly don the Redbirds logo. People don't "follow" the Cardinals or "keep up" with the Cardinals; they are fans of the Cardinals. And being a Cardinals fan is more than merely hating the Cubs to the north and the Royals to the west. It is more than merely wanting the men in red to win. It is more than a state of mind. It is a passion, a commitment of the baseball soul.

"There is something different about wearing a Cardinals uniform, and the different expectations of the fans who follow those players," noted the Man, who wore it with brilliance for 22 years. "They know the game, they understand the game, but most important, they love the game. And they love the Cardinals. You can't teach that. It has to come from the heart."

St. Louis is not just a great city with a great baseball franchise. St. Louis is baseball country, and the Cardinals are king of that country.

They Weren't Always the Cardinals

St. Louis fielded a team called the Browns or Brown Stockings in the National League when it began in 1876. In 1882, however, the Browns became a charter member of a new major league called the American Association. Curiously, the league was formed at least in part for cultural reasons. It offered beer and Sunday baseball to fans, two forbidden elements in the established National League.

The team's first president and one of its founders, Chris Von der Ahe, viewed the Browns (or Brown Stockings) not as a competitive sporting franchise that would proudly represent St. Louis, but as a source of customers for his city drinking establishment. Von der Ahe was soon bitten by the baseball bug, however, and eventually served as the team's manager. The team dominated the American Association for much of its tenure, and some claim Von der Ahe broke up the team after 1888 in the best interests of the league.

In any case, the fledgling American Association folded in 1891, and the St. Louis franchise was accepted into the National League beginning with the 1892 season. With Von der Ahe at the throttle, the Browns finished a woeful 56–94 in a split season. The remaining years of the 19th century were simply horrendous for the Browns, as the Stockings failed to post a single winning season until 1899 when the team managed an 84–67 mark. For the seven seasons from 1892 through 1898 the Browns were a ghastly 324 games under .500.

After the 56–94 opening campaign in 1892, the club went 57–75 in 1893 and 56–76 in 1894. From there, unbelievably, it actually got worse. In 1895 the Browns were 39–92 and followed that with a 40–90 log in 1896. The team bottomed out in 1897 with an unthinkable 29–102 record and "improved" to a 39–111 mark in 1898. Losses on the field spelled

By the
NUMBERS

7/11/1911—Date that the Federal Express of the New York, New Haven, and Hartford railroad was transporting the Cardinals to Boston when it jumped the track and fell down an 18-foot embankment near Bridgeport, Connecticut, taking the lives of 14 passengers. The team's Pullman cars had been near the front of the train, but when noise made sleeping difficult, manager Roger Bresnahan asked that the car be changed. The day coach that replaced the Cardinals' car was crushed in the mishap. The Cardinals players assisted in removing the bodies of the victims and rescuing the injured before switching to a special train that took them to Boston. The railroad paid the players $25 each for their services and as compensation for lost possessions.

defeats off the field as well. In 1898 Von der Ahe and his corporation declared bankruptcy, and with the NL planning to reduce its membership to eight teams (from a previous dozen) in 1899 (although it remained at twelve), the St. Louis Brown Stockings were staring into the muzzle of extinction.

Enter Frank and Stanley Robison, who operated a rather successful franchise in Cleveland called the Spiders. Feeling baseball would do better in the Missouri city, the two—with Frank as the point man—took over in St. Louis, buying the franchise at a sheriff's auction. They brought over a number of their Cleveland stars, including a pitcher named Cy Young. The move gutted the Spiders, and the team folded on the heels of a 20–134 mark in 1899.

The team's name was initially changed from Browns or Brown Stockings to Perfectos. That presumptuous name lasted just one season. With the club adorned in red-striped stockings and red-brimmed uniforms, *St. Louis Republic* sportswriter Willie McHale heard a woman fan remark, "What a lovely shade of cardinal." McHale used the nickname in his column, and it resonated with the fans so much that the name became official the following season, 1900.

The Robisons left their stamp on the Cardinals by renaming the team's stadium from League Park (previously Union Park) to Robison Field. The structure seated 15,200 in 1899, up from its 14,500 capacity of 1893. A disappointing 65–75 season in 1900 was followed by a 76–64 winner in 1901. That, however, was the high-water mark for the century's new decade. In 1902 the American League relocated a team to St. Louis and had them take the abandoned nickname Browns. Not only did the Robisons not have the city to themselves for very long, but that year the team began a nine-year drought, failing to post a single winning campaign until 1911, when it managed to finish a

What happened to the St. Louis Browns after 1902?

Answers to the trivia questions are on pages 161–162.

single game over .500 at 75–74. Even the 1911 crew had its low moments, however. On May 13 Fred Merkle of the Giants counted six RBIs in a single inning, as he and his fellow New Yorkers assaulted three Cardinals pitchers to the tune of 13 runs in the first inning en route to a 19–5 drubbing of the Redbirds. Giants skipper John McGraw, seeing a certain victory, lifted ace Christy Mathewson after he had pitched but one inning. Mathewson gave way to Rube Marquard, who fanned 14 Cardinals over the remaining eight innings for what was then an NL strikeout record by a reliever. Amazingly, the official scorer overlooked Rube Marquard's eight-inning brilliance in the 19–5 demolition of the Giants and credited Mathewson—who left after pitching the first inning—with the win.

Personnel decisions were not always wise. After the 1903 season, the Cubs' president, John Hart, traded veteran Chicago pitcher Jack Taylor to the Cardinals, believing that gambling was involved in his three losses to the White Sox in the postseason city series. Among the pitchers the Cardinals traded for Taylor was Hall of Famer Mordecai "Three Finger" Brown. Among the few happy moments of those early seasons were a four-games-to-three preseason triumph in a 1907 city series with the Browns. The Cardinals took a 5–2 verdict over the Browns in the fall of that year.

Prior to the 1902 season, Frank Robison committed another whopping, albeit amusing, blunder. On April 23 of that year he offered to put up the unheard-of sum of $10,000 to back his claim that the Pittsburgh Pirates would not repeat as NL champs. The Pirates players managed to assemble a pool of money to match Robison's challenge and then went out and won the pennant by 27½ games.

Madam Owner
and Better Times

Miraculously the team remained in St. Louis and in the less-than-competent hands of the Robison brothers. When Frank died in 1905 and Stanley in 1911, the ownership of the Cardinals was passed down to Frank's daughter, Helene Hathaway Britton, making her the first female owner of a major league baseball team. Ms. Britton was not a do-nothing executive. After the 1912 season she bought out the contract of manager Roger Bresnahan, who had run the team with minimal success beginning in 1909, and hired Miller Huggins as its pilot. Bresnahan, a Hall of Fame catcher, was far less effective in the dugout than he had been behind the plate. He posted a 255–352 mark during his four-year tenure, and so he was perhaps best known in his managerial days with the Cardinals for the $50,000 life insurance policy the team took out on him in 1909—largely for publicity purposes. And to the Cardinals' chagrin, he is even better known as the Yankees' Hall of Fame manager during the Babe Ruth era of the twenties.

Huggins' 1913 team finished dead last in the NL at 51–99. A best-ever 81–72 finish in 1914 for third place in the league was followed by two more losing seasons, and by 1916 Britton had had enough. She sold the team to her lawyer, James C. Jones, and a group of fan stockholders that included an automobile dealer named Sam Breadon.

The then fan-controlled Cardinals made a franchise-turning decision in 1917. The team hired Branch Rickey, who had been replaced as manager of the rival Browns, as team president. After an auspicious 82–70 season in 1917, the team continued to struggle on the field, turning in three consecutive losing seasons. By 1920 Breadon, who got his business start in the entertainment business vending popcorn at the St. Louis World's Fair in 1904, had turned his initial $200 invest-

Sam Breadon (right), majority owner of the Cardinals from 1920 to 1947, was instrumental in making it one of the game's best franchises. He is shown here with the Cardinals coach Mike Gonzalez (center) and manager Eddie Dyer (left).

ment in the Cardinals—made nearly 30 years before as a favor to a friend—into a majority ownership of the team, owning 72 percent of the shares. Breadon would prove to be a major figure in Cardinals history, skillfully and willfully directing the franchise through the 1947 season, when at age 71 he sold the team to Postmaster General Robert Hannegan and Fred Saigh. He died less than two years later.

Once in charge of the St. Louis franchise in 1920, Sam named himself president while wisely retaining Rickey—a minority owner—as vice president and general manager. (Rickey also managed the team from 1919 to 1925, after returning from a brief stint in the service

TRIVIA

What was Branch Rickey's nickname?

Answers to the trivia questions are on pages 161–162.

9

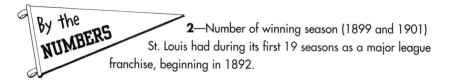

2—Number of winning season (1899 and 1901) St. Louis had during its first 19 seasons as a major league franchise, beginning in 1892.

during World War I.) Initially times were very hard. At its lowest point, the Cardinals' cashbox was all but empty. Things got so tight that the team was forced to wear used uniforms, and Breadon made a stock offering to raise funds. In 1920 the wily Breadon helped turn the financial corner by selling the inadequate wooden Robison Field and persuading Philip Ball, owner of the Browns, to let him move into Sportsman's Park, which remained the Cardinals' home for 33 seasons. Rickey used his wizardry by taking some of the money from the sale and bankrolling the Cardinals' first minor league affiliate in Houston, Texas, a move that signaled the beginning of a whole new era, one of building a successful major league franchise on a minor league foundation.

Although the team was still a year away from its first pennant, by 1925 the organization was on the ascendancy under the able leadership of Breadon and Rickey, posting winning seasons in four of the five years from 1921 to 1925. All the while things were happening just below the major league surface as well. In 1925 Rickey, whose keen eye for talent and uncanny ability to stretch a buck would serve Breadon and the Cardinals brilliantly through 1942, had amassed six farm teams, a number that would grow at a near-exponential rate in the coming years. Long-suffering Cardinals fans were soon to be rewarded with a baseball powerhouse, replete with Hall of Fame superstars, colorful characters, and, most important, championships.

The Rajah

A key to the team's upward thrust in the early half of the Roaring Twenties was the play of second baseman Rogers Hornsby. Born in Winters, Texas, in 1896, Hornsby broke into the majors in 1915 at the tender age of 19, hitting .246 in 18 games. No one could have imagined the impact he would have.

For the next four years, Hornsby was a very good, though not great, player, hitting between .281 and .327 and connecting on 27 home runs over the period. Then suddenly things changed. From 1920 to 1926 Hornsby averaged 210 hits per season for St. Louis. In 1921 his batting average skyrocketed to .397, and his home-run total reached 21. In addition, the 5'11", 175-pounder exploded for 126 RBIs. Great as it was, however, it was not even close to a career year. In 1922 Hornsby took home the Triple Crown, walloping a Ruthian 42 home runs, driving in an eye-popping 152 runs, and registering a .401 batting average. In 1924 Hornsby upped his batting mark to .424, the highest in the NL during the 20th century. The following year the 29-year-old superstar won his second Triple Crown on the strength of 39 homers, 143 RBIs, and a .403 batting mark in his first MVP season.

Hornsby stood back in the batter's box and delivered a level swing. When catchers tried to get him on low-and-away pitches, he used a diagonal stride to bring the offerings into his range. He had the most difficulty with pitches high and inside, as his stride brought him too close to the ball. Hornsby would lean away from those tosses, and often the umpire, out of respect for his keen batting eye, would call the pitch a ball. On the field Hornsby had a very mild, controlled manner. He rarely, if ever, argued umpires' calls and was never thrown out of a game.

Rogers Hornsby is second all time in batting average, with a .358 lifetime mark. He also won 701 games as a manager, most of which came when he was still playing.

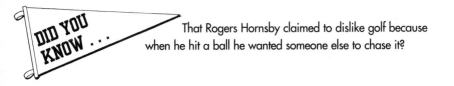

That Rogers Hornsby claimed to dislike golf because when he hit a ball he wanted someone else to chase it?

The handsome, dimpled, rosy-cheeked lad entered the Cardinals organization as a shortstop, had a brief stint at third, but eventually settled at second base. He became a solid defensive second sacker, despite difficulties going back in quest of short fly balls. The Rajah, as he was called, took extremely good care of himself. In an era of alcohol-fueled carousing, Hornsby neither smoked nor drank. He even abstained from coffee. Believing visual acuity to be a key to baseball excellence, he did not read or go to movies. And although Hornsby was known to be obsessed with conditioning, what with his no-smoke, no-drink, no-movies lifestyle, he did like to sleep and eat. He snoozed 11 to 12 hours per night, and his eating compulsion resulted in his gaining a great deal of weight in the off-season, perhaps a major reason he was essentially finished as a player by age 36. Throughout his career in baseball, he enjoyed sitting in hotel lobbies discussing hitting with anyone who would listen, never able to understand why those he engaged did not become as proficient with the bat as he was.

In 1926 few St. Louis residents were more popular than Hornsby, as the player/manager led his team to its first pennant. The Cardinals posted an 89–65 record, nipping the Cincinnati Reds by just two games. Spearheaded by Hornsby, Jim Bottomley, Les Bell, and NL MVP catcher Bob O'Farrell, St. Louis was a hitting juggernaut, leading the league in eight offensive categories. The World Series was now in view, with Babe Ruth and the New York Yankees as the opposition.

The Series was pure drama. The Cardinals took a two-games-to-one lead behind the pitching of right-hander Jesse Haines, and the Yankees headed for Sportsman's Park in a determined mood. The Bronx Bombers prevailed in Game 4, and then, on the strength of three homers by Ruth, forged ahead three games to two with a victory the following day in Game 5. With their backs touching the elimination wall, the Cardinals sent aging 39-year-old Grover Cleveland Alexander to the mound for Game 6. Alexander, a solitary man who said little and had a whispery voice when he did speak, came to the Cardinals early in the season and contributed nine wins to the St. Louis pennant push. Well past his prime and bedeviled by the maladies of alcoholism and epilepsy, "Pete" went the distance in a stirring 10–2 victory, his second complete-game victory of the Series.

Thinking his job was done, Alexander settled in to watch Game 7 from the bench. But in the seventh inning, with St. Louis clinging to a 3–2 lead, the Yankees loaded the bases. Hornsby decided to go to Alexander once more. Alexander managed to fan the dangerous Tony Lazzeri to close out the inning and then put down New York in order in the eighth. With but one out left in the game, Alexander walked Ruth and put the tying run on first. Having stolen successfully in Game 6, the Bambino took off in an attempt to get into scoring position once again. Bob O'Farrell sent a missile to Hornsby, who slapped a tag on the Yankees slugger to end the Series and make the St. Louis Cardinals world champions.

Despite the euphoria of the moment, all was not well below the Cardinals surface. The strong-willed Breadon had had a bellyful of Hornsby. Despite his model conduct on the field, the Rajah had an icy, sharp, brutally blunt side to him. Even worse, the contentious Hornsby had a belligerent attitude toward authority figures. He would order front-office people out of the clubhouse, telling them to stay away from his players and mind their own business. And if they didn't like it, they could bring in someone else as manager.

And that is exactly what Breadon did. On the heels of a nasty contract dispute in which the player/manager wanted a three-year pact at the then-incredible sum of $50,000 per season, the frugal Breadon pulled the trigger. In an absolutely stunning move, he dispatched Hornsby to the New York Giants in a two-for-one swap, which brought future Hall of Famer Frankie Frisch and pitcher Jimmy Ring to the Cardinals. An enraged Hornsby engaged his nasty side once more after the trade. He strung the nervous Breadon out for top dollar by cashing in the 1,167 shares of Cardinals stock he owned. Hornsby settled for $112,000, a ransom note for which the Cardinals paid $86,000, the Giants $12,000, and every other NL club $2,000.

Leaving St. Louis did not prove to be a panacea for the Rajah. The outspoken, uncompromising Hornsby remained abrasive and hypercritical to the end. Having an arrogant, racist streak, he saw little, if any, value in his players and earned the contempt of legions of players he managed or coached. The best he would say of Mickey Mantle, for example, was that "he looks like a major league ballplayer." Though performing with brilliance on the field, Hornsby—with his near-compulsive rudeness—continued to accumulate enemies among players and owners in virtually every city in which he was employed. At age 66 his final job in baseball was as coach under Casey Stengel for the hapless (40–120) 1962 New York Mets. He died a year later.

TRIVIA

Who played the role of Grover Cleveland Alexander in the Hollywood film *The Winning Team*?
BONUS QUESTION:
Although the 1926 Series ended with an unsuccessful steal, how was the final out recorded in the movie?

Answers to the trivia questions are on pages 161–162.

The Curse of the Bottle

Many years ago, a major league manager said that any skipper who tells you he does not know two or three guys with a drinking problem is lying. Whoever had Grover Cleveland Alexander on his club knew he had at least one player with a severe alcohol problem.

You just have to wonder how good a pitcher "Pete" Alexander might have been had he conquered that "ol' demon rum," as they put it at the time. The man pitched only three and a half years for the Cardinals—another example in a long list of absolutely brilliant player moves made by the matchless Branch Rickey—when he was already 39 years old and managed to win 55 games while losing just 34. He completed 48 games after he was 40 years old. Joining the Cardinals from the Cubs late in the 1926 campaign, Alexander figured in three of the team's four World Series wins, winning two and saving one. He had an ERA of 0.89 over 20 innings.

Those Cardinals numbers alone are enough for a pitcher to feel rather satisfied with his career. The 6'1", 185-pound Alexander, however, had already won 318 games before joining the Redbirds. In 2001 Bill James, maven of baseball statistical analysis, declared Alexander the third-best pitcher of all time, behind only Walter Johnson and Lefty Grove. James notes that biographers frequently attribute Alexander's alcoholism to his being gassed in a World War I training procedure. This is pure myth. Alcoholism is known to run in families, and it flowed freely within Alexander's familial network. His father and grandfather were heavy drinkers, and Alexander was renowned as a drinker prior to 1918. Alexander suffered from the disease throughout his life and was known to drink his wife's perfume when liquor was not available.

Alcoholism was not his only demon. Alexander also had epilepsy, a brain disorder that occurs when electrical signals from the brain are disrupted. It results in physical seizures. A beaning that Alexander suffered early in his career may have contributed to his epilepsy, because the disability can be brought on by severe brain injuries. Pete was struck in the head by a shortstop's throw as he was attempting to break up a double play in a Central Association game in Galesburg, Illinois. Alexander was unconscious for 56 hours and suffered blurred vision for a while thereafter. In addition, Pete experienced what is now called post-traumatic stress disorder after World War I. We know, for example, that a shell exploded so close to him that it robbed him of his hearing in one ear. In any case, the combination of alcoholism, epilepsy, and stress reactions had a devastating effect on the great pitcher's life. In 1925, a year before joining the Cardinals, he was admitted to a sanitarium.

Rumors of Alexander's drinking harken back to the 1915 World Series when he was with the Phillies. After going 31–10 with a league-leading 1.22 ERA, he won the Series opener against Boston by a 3–1 score on October 8. He returned three days later and turned in another gem, losing 2–1 in the bottom of the ninth. When the Phillies fell again the following day, and trailed Boston 3–1 through four games, Phillies manager Pat Moran tabbed Alexander to start Game 6 on October 13.

He didn't. Moran inexplicably switched to Erskine Mayer at the last minute. Mayer lasted little more than two innings, giving way to—not Alexander—but Eppa Rixey, in what turned out to be an agonizing 5–4 loss. The word on the street was that Pete was so drunk he was unable to take the mound in the critical game. Alexander, of course, vehemently denied the charge. Perhaps the allegation is without merit, but the last-second shift by Moran in such a do-or-die situation is, well, curious.

Surprisingly, when he emerged from the sanitarium for the 1926 season, Alexander was not treated with the disdain that was characteristic of how alcoholics were regarded. Instead he was given a day in his honor, a new car, and a hefty $5,500 contract. It had taken 11 years for

DID YOU KNOW . . . That Alexander was one of only two players named after United States presidents? The other was Franklin Delano Roosevelt Wiend, who pitched for the Reds in 1958 and 1960. Alexander, however, was the only player to be portrayed by a United States president, Ronald Reagan in the 1952 movie *The Winning Team*.

Grover Cleveland Alexander joined the Cardinals at age 39, late in the 1926 season, and went on to win 55 games over parts of four seasons. An epileptic who also battled drinking problems, Alexander, remarkably, recorded 48 complete games after the age of 40.

Alexander to redeem himself before followers of the national pastime. And redeem himself he did, much to the delight of Cardinals fans. Ironically, Alexander sort of stumbled to the mound when called upon by Frisch to relieve in the final game, leaving legions

TRIVIA

For which team did Alexander pitch prior to going to St. Louis?

Answers to the trivia questions are on pages 161–162.

of fans thinking that Alex the Great was back to his old ways, deep in the bag after pitching so well earlier. Not so. He may have been suffering from a seizure or even been a tad hung over, but he was not drunk. He pitched magnificently.

That was Alexander's last national hurrah. He did appear in the 1928 World Series after winning 16 games that season, but he fared poorly. He pitched in and lost one game and was hit for 11 earned runs in just five innings.

As with many alcoholics, Alexander's end was not pretty. Out of dollars and friends who might have helped him find a more stable occupation, the introverted Alexander was forced to appear at carnivals and in sideshows as a novelty after his career was over. He died alone in a boarding house in his hometown of St. Paul, Minnesota, at age 63.

The questions remain: How would Alexander have fared in contemporary times? Would his alcoholism have been regarded as a disease? Would he have entered a recovery program? Would his epilepsy have been controlled in a medically sound fashion? Would Alex the Great have been even greater? There are no certain answers to the medical questions, but as to the final one, it is hard to imagine how he could have been any greater.

One of a Kind

If Sam Breadon was the backbone of the Cardinals, team president Wesley Branch Rickey was the team's brain.

Rickey began his career in baseball as an undistinguished catcher, breaking in with the St. Louis Browns in 1905. The 5'9", 175-pound Rickey appeared in 120 games, hitting just .239 in 343 official at-bats. He was no bargain behind the plate either. The Washington Senators once stole 13 bases in a single game with Rickey catching for the New York Highlanders (later the Yankees). An arm injury put a merciful end to his brief playing career.

He fared little better as a manager, compiling a 597–664 record over a 10-season span in St. Louis with the Browns and Cardinals. He managed to register a winning record only three times, from 1921 to 1923, with the Cardinals, and was relieved of his dugout duties in favor of Rogers Hornsby by owner Sam Breadon after winning 13 of 38 games in 1925.

Honoring a vow he had made to his mother, Rickey did not go to the park on Sundays. He would not even carry his equipment to the train depot if Sunday was a getaway day. Later, as a manager and executive, he continued his practice of strictly observing the Sabbath by using managerial substitutes on Sundays. The pious Methodist neither drank nor cursed, allowing himself an occasional "Judas Priest!" as his most vile expletive. Incredibly literate, Rickey was a lover of philosophy, holder of a law degree from the University of Michigan, and verbally gifted. He regularly spoke at boys' clubs and Christian organizations.

Rickey, however, was an enigmatic man. Despite his walk-the-walk piety, the man with the bushy eyebrows who sported bow ties and big cigars was as slick as any hustler of his era. With the air of a con man, Rickey had no equal in player transactions. He was simply brilliant in snookering players into signing contracts at bargain salaries. Joe Garagiola once said of him, "It was easy to figure out Mr. Rickey's thinking about contracts. He had both players and money, and just didn't like to see the two of them mix." Moreover, he had an incredible eye for talent, seeing the untapped potential in George Sisler and Dizzy Dean, and the hidden skills in Billy Cox and Preacher Roe. He was also a veritable baseball actuary, able to calculate with uncommon precision just how much productivity a veteran player had left.

As such, he would skin his trading partners like rubes, leaving those rival executives with the impression that he was doing them a favor. He entered every deal aware of which players he desired and which players he would give up. One of his favorite ploys was to hold back the player he most wanted to trade in the initial stages of negotiation, offering a player he wanted to retain instead. Thinking they were outfoxing

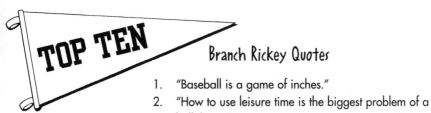

TOP TEN Branch Rickey Quotes

1. "Baseball is a game of inches."
2. "How to use leisure time is the biggest problem of a ballplayer."
3. "I don't care if I was a ditch-digger at a dollar a day, I'd want to do my job better than the fellow next to me. I'd want to be the best at whatever I do."
4. "It is not the honor you take with you, but the heritage you leave behind."
5. "Luck is the residue of design."
6. "Problems are the price you pay for progress."
7. "The greatest untapped reservoir of raw material in the history of our game is the black race."
8. "The man with the ball is responsible for what happens to the ball."
9. "Trade a player a year too early rather than a year too late."
10. "Never play checkers with the man who carries his own board."

TRIVIA

Branch Rickey broke the National League color line in 1947. What executive did the same in the American League, and who was the player?

Answers to the trivia questions are on pages 161–162.

Rickey, opposing executives would then seek out the held-back player, never realizing that they had fallen into one of his psychological traps.

The Cardinals simply flourished with Rickey as president, posting 15 winning seasons and claiming six pennants and four world championships over the final 17 years of a front-office tenure that ended in 1942. Individual players also flourished under him. As Roy Campanella put it, "He made me a better catcher, a better person on and off the field. He made me a completely changed individual."

Despite Rickey's talent-assessment acumen and trading savvy, he was best known as the virtual inventor of the modern-day farm system. At one point he had 32 minor league teams and 600 players undergirding the major league Cardinals. An organizational wizard, Rickey assembled a network of managers, coaches, and scouts to ready the farmhands for big-league duty. The Cardinals' system became so powerful that for 25 years the Cardinals never had to "buy" a player from another team. Rickey's system was so formidable that in 1937 Commissioner Landis actually "freed" 91 Cardinals minor leaguers. Rickey profited directly from these dealings, earning a percentage of the price at which a player was sold.

Forced out of the Cardinals organization by a jealous associate after the 1942 season, the 61-year-old's best baseball days were actually still ahead. In 1945 he signed on with the Brooklyn Dodgers as president and general manager. There Rickey not only established the Dodgers' vaunted farm system, but at age 66 pulled the ultimate coup: breaking the baseball color line with the signing of Jackie Robinson. Robinson, after Rickey's death years later, looked back on their relationship: "I realized how much our relationship had deepened after I left baseball. It was that later relationship that made me feel almost as if I had lost my own father. Branch Rickey, especially after I was no longer in the sports spotlight, treated me like a son."

Giant that he was, Rickey did not gain entrance into the Hall of Fame until 1967, two years after his death, when the Veterans Committee voted him in.

Few front-office personnel have affected the game the way Branch Rickey (left) did, shown here with pitcher Paul Dean. Rickey created the modern farm system as vice president of the Cardinals and helped to integrate baseball when he signed Jackie Robinson to play for the Dodgers.

Good Times

Coming off 1926, much was expected from the Cardinals. Breadon, having dispatched Hornsby to the Giants, was aware of the rising expectations.

The 1927 campaign was full of good news and bad news. The good news was that the Cardinals won 92 and lost 61 under Bob O'Farrell, the league's MVP the previous season. That was a three-and-a-half-game improvement over the 1926 world championship squad. Fiery Frankie Frisch filled in ably at second, diminishing, at least somewhat, the void created by the absence of the Rajah. Other stars such as O'Farrell, Jim Bottomley, and Chick Hafey turned in solid seasons in the field, while Jesse Haines and Alexander had 20-win seasons to lead the pitching. The bad news was that St. Louis finished a game and a half behind Pittsburgh in their quest for another opportunity to shine in the fall classic.

The Series sabbatical lasted just one year, as the Cardinals won the 1928 pennant with an even better 95–59 mark. New skipper Bill McKechnie had moved up from O'Farrell's coaching staff. Bottomley, with his .325 average, was the league's MVP, and the starting pitching staff proved iron-like, turning in 83 complete games. After nearly 40 years of wandering in the major league baseball desert, the Cardinals, with two pennants in three seasons, ruled as the lords of the city's entertainment world. The year closed on a sour note, however, as St. Louis was swept in four by the potent Yankees.

The stock market crashed in 1929, and the Redbirds nearly did as well, going a mediocre 78–74, en route to a fourth-place finish in the Senior Circuit. That a four-games-over-.500 year would be declared mediocre or disappointing bears testimony to how powerful the St. Louis franchise had become.

Outfielder Chick Hafey (left) and first baseman Jim Bottomley (right) were two of four future Hall of Famers who led the Cardinals' resurgence in the twenties (Hornsby and pitcher Jesse Haines were the other two).

With Gabby Street at the helm, the team rebounded in the first year of the new decade, ringing up 92 wins against 62 defeats. It was an exciting campaign, to say the least. The Cardinals were 53–52 on August 8, in fourth place, 12 games out. From there, the team went berserk, winning 39 of its final 49 games and taking a three-game set from Brooklyn in late September to pull into the lead. The battle, however, was with the Cubs, one that was not decided until the second-to-last game of the season. In the World Series the Cardinals fell in six games to the Philadelphia Athletics.

The team emerged undaunted from the World Series disappointment of 1930 by blowing the doors off the NL in 1931, with a 101–53 mark. Second baseman Frankie Frisch was the league's MVP as the club clinched the pennant on September 16 behind Bill Hallahan's 18th win of the campaign, 6–3 over the Phillies. At the same time, the Reds trimmed

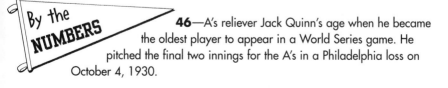

By the NUMBERS

46—A's reliever Jack Quinn's age when he became the oldest player to appear in a World Series game. He pitched the final two innings for the A's in a Philadelphia loss on October 4, 1930.

All-Twenties
Cardinals Team

Position	Player
First Base	Jim Bottomley
Second Base	Rogers Hornsby
Third Base	Les Bell
Shortstop	Specs Toporcer
Left Field	Chick Hafey
Center Field	Taylor Douthit
Right Field	Jack Smith
Pitcher	Jesse Haines
Catcher	Bob O'Farrell
Manager	Rogers Hornsby

the Giants twice, 7–3 and 4–3. The A's repeated in the AL to set up what figured to be an exciting World Series rematch. It was. The A's took the first game of the Series, but the Redbirds answered by winning the next two. After the A's took the fourth game, Cardinals ace Bill Hallahan chucked a 5–1 win to put St. Louis within a game of their second world championship. Game 6, however, went to the A's in Sportsman's Park. It was down to an all-or-nothing seventh game. The Cardinals jumped out to an early 4–0 advantage but needed a clutch relief performance from Hallahan to hold off the A's, 4–2. The Series hitting star proved to be the other half of the Cardinals' keystone combination: combative shortstop Pepper Martin batted .500, while scoring and driving in five runs.

The Cardinals were becoming an NL dynasty, with no end in sight. The team averaged more than 90 wins per season from 1926 through 1931, finishing first or second every year except 1929. Moreover, St. Louis took four pennants and two World Series. The team was directed by Sam Breadon and personnel master Branch Rickey. Breadon was tough-minded, Rickey decisive and unswerving. "I did not mind the public criticism," Rickey once reflected. "That sort of thing has not changed any program I thought was good." He was also able to keep sentimentality out of the decision-making process. "It [a baseball box score] doesn't tell how big you are, what church you attend, what color you are, or how your father voted in the last election," he once pontificated. "It just tells what kind of baseball player you were on that particular day."

Rickey, however, found a way to put a lot of players on the field who were good on many days. Indeed, stars dotted the team roster. Hall of

Famers Jim Bottomley, Grover Cleveland Alexander, Burleigh Grimes, Dizzy Dean, Jesse Haines, Rogers Hornsby, Chick Hafey, and Frankie Frisch all spent some time in Cardinals Red during those years. And the Cardinals were providing much more than entertaining baseball for their adoring fans. They were offering St. Louis a delightful diversion from the pain of the Great Depression. This was a pre-TV era, one in which baseball was the only truly big-league sport. In fact, listening to one's favorite team on the radio was, for many Americans, the favorite pastime. Hence, Cardinals baseball was important for cultural as well as sporting reasons. The game was greatly affected by the Depression. The Cardinals, for example, wore uniforms that were often torn and dirty, and player salaries plummeted by 25 percent between 1929 and 1933. Anyone fortunate enough to be a member of a major league team had much for which to be thankful, as jobs were scarce in the all-too-real world off the diamond.

While Americans—perched between two world wars—suffered through the ravages of the pre–New Deal economic collapse, Cardinals fans could at least take comfort in rooting for a baseball team that would give them the scent of success amid all the grim failures of a nation in crisis. As tough as things became, they could still occasionally forget their worries and root home a Redbirds win.

At least that's the way it looked in the early thirties. Baseball, however—as Joe Garagiola put it—is a funny game. Just as the Cardinals appeared nearly

TRIVIA

Which two players dominated the home run and RBI production of the twenties Cardinals?

Answers to the trivia questions are on pages 161–162.

unconquerable, their fortunes cooled. Inexplicably, the team played sub-.500 ball in 1932, turning in a 72–82 season. They followed that with a better but unimpressive 82–71 campaign in 1933. The two lackluster campaigns brought Gabby Street's tenure as manager to an end. On July 24 he was replaced by second sacker Frankie Frisch.

There was concern in Cardinalville that the team's championship days may have evaporated along with the drops of champagne spilled in celebration of the 1931 season extraordinaire, but the most exciting year—if not the best—was yet to come.

The Fordham Flash

Frank Francis "Frankie" Frisch was a dynamite athlete and a star at Fordham University in New York. Though only 5'11" and 165 pounds, Frisch excelled in baseball, football, basketball, and track. As a college graduate, Frisch was a bit of an anomaly among the hardscrabble, tobacco-spitting crowd that populated major league rosters. Nonetheless, baseball had to be his first professional choice because when he graduated in 1919 it was America's only big-league sport.

Frisch's skills were evident in that he was immediately accepted by the New York Giants on their major league roster. And the Giants were no ordinary team. They were managed by John McGraw, whose demanding nature and hunger for victory would rival any of today's NFL head coaches. McGraw drove the young Frisch to greatness, tutoring him endlessly in hitting and base-running techniques, ever aware of young Frankie's speed and dexterity. Perhaps owing to Frisch's intelligence, as well as his hustle and drive, McGraw soon named Frisch captain.

Though Frisch was a second baseman by trade, McGraw employed his young athlete at shortstop or even third base if he felt Frisch could help the New Yorkers there. The jump from college to the majors was a long one, and it took Frisch—who hit .226 and .280 in his first two campaigns—until 1921, when the Fordham Flash hit .341, scored 121 runs, and batted in 100 more, to achieve hitting brilliance. From the outset, however, his fielding was excellent and his speed scintillating. By 1921 he led the NL in stolen bases with 48. Extremely difficult to strike out, Frisch never hit below .314 from 1921 to 1926 and helped the Giants to four consecutive pennants beginning in 1921.

Things turned sour for Frankie in New York after 1924, however, when the Giants—particularly in 1926 with a fifth-place finish in the

Frankie Frisch had a college degree, an anomaly for baseball players at the time, and came to the Cardinals after a successful career with the Giants. He was maestro of the thirties Cardinals, leading them on the field and as manager.

That Frisch struck out just 272 times in 9,112 at-bats?

NL—drifted toward mediocrity. McGraw began venting on his hotly competitive leader and then, at the close of the 1926 season, peddled him to the Cardinals in the deal involving Rogers Hornsby. The trade put enormous pressure on the switch-hitting Frisch. Not only had Hornsby won an insane six straight batting titles (averaging .397 in the process), but the Cardinals had just won their first world championship.

Undaunted, Frisch headed for St. Louis, promptly hitting .337 and setting records in the field for chances and assists at second base while leading the league in fielding percentage. He finished second in MVP balloting to champion Pittsburgh's "Big Poison," Paul Waner. The following season St. Louis, with Frisch as the team leader, won the pennant, and four years later he was the MVP of a world champion Cardinals team.

It didn't end there. Frisch became the team's playing manager in 1933 and piloted the club to another World Series triumph in that role. He remained the Cardinals skipper until 1938, one year after ending his playing career at age 39. Frisch was a showman. Fiery, combative, and colorful, he loved to argue with, show up, and needle umpires. By 1934 he was the main-stage performer among a host of colorful characters, including Dizzy Dean, Pepper Martin, Ripper Collins, Joe "Ducky" Medwick, and Leo Durocher.

Frisch finished his career with 2,880 hits and a .316 average, stealing 419 bases and being elected to the Hall of Fame in 1947.

Frisch went on to manage the Pittsburgh Pirates from 1940 to 1946—where he once was ejected by Hall of Fame umpire Jocko Conlan for coming out on the field with an umbrella in quest of a rainout—and the Cubs from 1949 to 1951, never again winning a pennant.

He also did several stints as an announcer, during which time he referred to himself as the Ol' Flash. He respected the skills and adored the

TRIVIA

For what controversial activity among baseball award-granting was Frisch well known?

Answers to the trivia questions are on pages 161–162.

personality of Yogi Berra, and he collected Yogiisms before the practice became commonplace. He once quoted Yogi complaining about the size of a house, remarking it was "awful full of rooms." He also noted Berra's wonder as to why his attractive, eventual wife, Carmen, could have been interested in "a mug like him." "I ain't sure because all of our dates have been at night," theorized Yogi. "She ain't seen me in the daylight."

Frisch became very well known for his efforts behind the microphone. Among his Frischisms were the following: "Oh, those bases on balls . . ."; "Going, going, gone . . ."; and "Socko" and "Slam a lam a ding dong" (for home runs).

Frisch offered other memorable witticisms. Lamenting the loss of colorful characters in the national game, he claimed baseball "needs some good old Tabasco sauce to give it the old time kick." He once noted that strikeout-prone slugger Dave Nicholson "whiffs like a saloon door." He hated knuckleballs, claiming they were an "old-man's-home pitch for guys with Weary Willie arms."

TRIVIA

> When Frisch left as Cardinals manager in 1938, only one man had been in the dugout longer. Who was he?

Answers to the trivia questions are on pages 161–162.

Later, noting the effectiveness of Hall of Famer Hoyt Wilhelm's "old-man's-home" pitch, Frisch was more charitable, labeling it "a tricky pitch with a will of its own." He didn't think much, however, of the fly ball savvy of Yankees and Athletics infielder and outfielder Hector Lopez, observing that Lopez "looked like he was having dizzy spells when he went after a fly ball."

Yearning for the old grind 'em out, spikes high days, Frisch mocked the use of batting helmets. "If we must have helmets," he remarked, "how about the one with a spike in the top—such as Kaiser Wilhelm's tough soldiers wore in World War I?"

Frisch would plug his sponsor by integrating its name into the action. Stealing bases "was as easy as riding into third in a car greased with Quaker State Motor Oil," in a play he worked with teammate Ross Youngs in 1922.

Always self-effacing despite his brilliance as a player, Frisch claimed to hold "a record that will never be topped . . . I fanned on six pitches, three on one side of the plate, three on the other . . . and never moved my bat."

The Gashouse Gang

The 1934 season proved magical in St. Louis. Not only did the Cardinals inch themselves ahead of the New York Giants with Bill Terry, Mel Ott, and Carl Hubbell, winning the pennant by just two games with a 95–58 record, but they did it with as colorful a collection of players as has ever won a championship in any sport. The 1934 season was the year of the famous Gashouse Gang.

Of course there was the spirited team leader and manager, second sacker Frankie Frisch, who was about the only man alive who could make Cardinals fans forget about the banishment of the Rajah. Playing to Frisch's right at third was harmonica-playing Pepper Martin, whose speed was attributed to a childhood spent chasing rabbits in Oklahoma and undoubtedly helped him to capture the 1934 record for stolen bases. Between Frisch and Martin was the shortstop, none other than "the Lip," Leo Durocher. At first base stood the great James Anthony Collins, better known as Ripper, who hit .333, blasting 35 home runs, knocking in 128 tallies, and tying Mel Ott for the 1934 home-run title. The outfield included a young Joe "Ducky" Medwick, who would later claim a Triple Crown.

Collins would have been a worthy MVP choice were it not for one Jay Hanna "Dizzy" Dean, who managed a league-leading 30 wins against just seven defeats and a 2.66 ERA. Dean did not confine himself to being a starter. He appeared in an astounding 50 games, throwing 312 innings, and saved 7 games. The 24-year-old Dean was a man of uncommon good humor and boundless confidence. His 20-year-old brother, Paul—known as "Daffy"—was a promising rookie. Prior to the season Dizzy boldly predicted 45 victories between the two brothers. The elder Dean exulted in his brother's skills and strongly endorsed the

The Cardinals defeated the Tigers in the 1934 World Series four games to three. Game 7, in Detroit, was won handily by the Cardinals, 11–0, but Joe Medwick (above) had to be removed from the game in the sixth inning when the crowd started pelting him with fruit and bottles.

youth's capabilities to anyone who might doubt Paul's capacity to hold up his end of his boastful brother's claim. "Nah, don't worry about Paul none," he once stated. "He may even be a greater pitcher than me, if that's possible."

Dizzy's prophesy was more than fulfilled. With Paul notching 19 victories, the Deans contributed not 45, but 49 wins to the Redbirds' total. Their combined wins that season were the most ever for a brother combination. And over the course of their Cardinals careers they would combine for 180 wins—Dizzy with 154 and Paul 46.

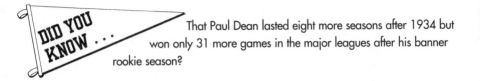

Despite the team's brilliance the 1934 season was high drama. On September 14, St. Louis found itself five and a half games in arrears of the hard-charging New Yorkers. The Deans then delivered to close the gap. A week later the Cardinals took down the Brooklyn Dodgers twice behind Dizzy's gem in the opener and a no-hitter by Paul in the nightcap. "How would you feel?" groaned the "Old Perfesser," Dodgers skipper Casey Stengel. "You get three itsy-bitsy hits off the big brother in the first game, and then you look around and there's the little brother with biscuits from the same table to throw at you."

The race went down to the candle's wick, with Dizzy winning the final game of the season and setting up a confrontation between the Cardinals and the Detroit Tigers. The Tigers, winners of 101 games, were loaded, sporting the likes of Mickey Cochrane, Charlie Gehringer, and mighty Hank Greenberg.

In Game 4, Dean raced out to pinch run for Virgil "Spud" Davis. What began as an enthusiastic sprint down to second ended in tense drama as Dean was hit squarely in the head by a throw from Tigers shortstop Billy Rogell, dropping him as if he had been hit by an elephant gun. Somehow Dizzy summoned his wits sufficiently to pitch in Game 5 and, more important, in the do-or-die seventh game.

Elden Auker faced "the Great Dean" in the deciding game. Dean had won an earlier game, and his brother Paul rang up the other Cardinals wins. Auker had split his two Series decisions up to that point. The game, which figured to be exciting and intense, proved to be the latter. The game itself was a bust, but a dramatic occurrence within the contest will be a part of baseball and Gashouse lore forever. St. Louis led 7–0 in the sixth inning when Ducky Medwick seared a line drive to center and slammed into third base with spikes aloft as Tigers third baseman Marv Owen held up his glove as if he was going to apply a tag. Owen brought his foot down and dug his spikes into Medwick's leg. An enraged Medwick

TRIVIA

Which famous woman athlete actually pitched an inning for the Cardinals in a 1934 exhibition game?

Answers to the trivia questions are on pages 161–162.

kicked back, the two players tangled, and when the dugouts emptied, the rumble was on. After the players had been cleared from the field and emotions had been brought under control, Medwick offered his hand to Owen as a token of peaceful resolution. The angry Tiger would have none of it and refused to shake hands. The Cardinals answered with the bat, as Collins made the score 9–0 by delivering Medwick a moment later.

When Medwick assumed his position in left, seventeen thousand incensed Motor City fans, with clenched fists, pelted him with insults and debris. Commissioner Landis intervened, ordering Medwick from the game for the safety of all. After a 17-minute respite, the Cardinals went on to win 11–0 behind a superb performance by Dean.

The Cardinals were world champions once again.

Dizzy

He won only 150 big-league games in a career that, although spanning a dozen years, contained but six largely full seasons. Yet no member of the famed Gashouse Gang was more popular and is more memorable than Jerome Hanna "Dizzy" Dean, an incredible right-hander from Lucas, Arkansas. Dizzy Dean was a big man by the standards of his time, but by no means a giant—listed at 6'2", 182 pounds. He made his debut in 1930, throwing a three-hitter for a 3–1 victory on the final day of the season. Dean, whose lifetime record was a modest 39–33 through 1933, became a baseball behemoth the following year, winning 30 games in the regular season and two more in the World Series. He led the league in strikeouts, mostly due to a powerful fastball called the "fogger." Dean was "foggin' 'em past dizzier batters' heads," according to Gashouse wordsmith Frankie Frisch.

His antics were colorful, crass, and controversial. "When Ol' Diz was out there pitching," recounted fellow Gashouse prankster Pepper Martin, "it was more than just another ballgame. It was a regular three-ring circus, and everybody was wide-awake and enjoying being alive." Prior to the magical 1934 Cardinals carpet ride, the free-spirited Dean skipped an exhibition game, an act so grievous at the time that Branch Rickey testified against the pitching ace in the office of Commissioner Landis.

The irrepressible Dean was a man of boundless confidence. "Anybody who's ever had the privilege of seeing me play," he once said, "knows that I am the greatest pitcher in the world." After the final game of the season, with the Cardinals clinching the 1934 pennant in a tense run against the Giants, the bold ace—amid the wild celebrations in Sportsman's Park—instructed a young boy to place a four-pound block of ice on the pitching rubber. When the youth was asked why he was to

DID YOU KNOW . . . That from 1933 through 1936, Dean appeared in 199 games, pitched 1,244 innings, completed 107 games, won 102, and saved 27 more? This was after pitching 286 innings in 46 games in 1932.

perform this unusual chore, he said, "Dizzy told me this morning to put it there after the game; he said it would be burning up if I didn't."

The youth was a believer. "Go ahead, feel it." he said. "Even the ice hasn't gotten it cooled yet." Dean was a believer, too, and felt any charge of arrogance was unjust. "It ain't braggin'," he explained, "if you can back it up."

In the fourth game of the Series, the pinch-running Dizzy was beaned by a throw from Tigers shortstop Billy Rogell that felled Dean "like a marionette whose string had snapped." Fans feared for the zany pitcher's very life as he lay motionless on the diamond. Though almost certainly apocryphal, newspaper headlines allegedly reported the following day: X-Rays of Dean's Head Show Nothing. That such a yarn even made it into circulation is indicative of how the media regarded the amusing ace. As for Dean's attitude concerning the long-term effects of the injury, his response to the question as to whether he would pitch as scheduled in Game 5 leaves nothing to question. Of course he would pitch: "You can't hurt no Dean by hittin' him on the head."

Though beaten 3–1 on a home run by Charlie Gehringer, Dean was unfazed as he approached Game 7. When he dropped by the Tigers' bullpen before the game, he said to Detroit starter Elden Auker, "You don't expect to get anyone out with that stuff, do you?"

Auker got few out as the Cardinals scored 11 times, while the matchless Dean shut out the American League champs, a team that scored a breathtaking 958 runs in 154 regular-season games.

Dizzy followed his 1934 mastery—a year in which he claimed MVP honors—with a 28–12 season in 1935 and a strong 24–13 campaign in 1936. He was beaten out for the MVP in 1935 by Cubs

TRIVIA

Which Hall of Fame pitcher, similar to Dean, had only 165 wins, the bulk of which (97) he won in four great seasons?

Answers to the trivia questions are on pages 161–162.

A raw, unpolished talent when he came to the majors from the hills of Arkansas, Dizzy Dean won 30 games and the MVP in 1934, 134 games overall for the Cards, and the everlasting affection of baseball fans everywhere.

17—Dizzy Dean's uniform number.

great Gabby Hartnett and by the Giants' master Carl Hubbell the following year. When he was in his prime, there was no one quite like Dizzy Dean. "You were attracted by the graceful rhythm of his pitching motion," noted the editor of *The New York Times*, "the long majestic sweep of his arm as he let the ball fly, the poised alertness after the pitch. That was what counted, and you knew it when batter after batter swung ineptly at pitches they couldn't even see."

"Son," Dizzy would ask a tormented hitter, "what kind of pitch would you like to miss?" And it was all raw talent. "As a ballplayer, Dean was a natural phenomenon, like the Grand Canyon or the Great Barrier Reef," wrote the greatest of sports columnists, Red Smith. "Nobody ever taught him baseball, and he never had to learn. He was just doing what came naturally when a scout named Don Curtis discovered him on a Texas sandlot and gave him his first contract."

After three brilliant seasons, the exhausted Dean, seemingly en route to another 25-win season, wanted to sit out the 1937 All-Star Game but changed his mind at the urging of Cardinals owner Sam Breadon. It was an unfortunate decision for Dizzy, as the Cardinals ace was hit on the foot by a screaming line drive off the bat of Earl Averill, breaking a toe. Refusing to allow for complete healing, Dean had to adjust his pitching motion when he returned to the rotation prematurely. Only 27, Dizzy's early return was more than a mistake. It was a baseball tragedy. Dean developed a bursitis-ridden sore arm that eventually ended his career.

Rickey sagely traded him to the Chicago Cubs for the then-unthinkable sum of $185,000 and three players for the 1938 season. Dizzy—then sporting a dazzling curve and rhythm-thwarting changeup in place of his once burning fogger—managed to win seven of eight decisions for the pennant-winning Chicagoans. Despite the 7–1 log, however, Dean's career was clearly facing extinction as he threw just 75 innings that season. From 1939 to 1941 Dean won only nine and lost seven, pitching just 150 innings—fewer than half as many as he worked in the incredible 1934 campaign. The 1941 season was essentially his final season. He was only 31 years old.

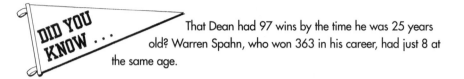

That Dean had 97 wins by the time he was 25 years old? Warren Spahn, who won 363 in his career, had just 8 at the same age.

Six years later Dean added to his legend by coming out of retirement for the hapless, publicity-starved St. Louis Browns after repeatedly criticizing the Browns' struggling hurlers. Dean allowed three hits and a walk but no earned runs in the final game of the season. He even contributed a hit of his own. With that, however, Jerome Hanna Dean's day in the sun as an active player was over.

Ever the prankster and humorist as a player, Dean entertained legions of baseball fans while horrifying grammarians by slaughtering the English language for 20 years as an announcer. "He slud into third" was a typical grammatical transgression that might set more eloquent Americans on edge. Dean, however, remained unaffected. "Let the teachers teach English," he allowed, "and I will teach baseball. There is a lot of people in the United States who say *isn't* and they ain't eating."

As for his linguistic version of *sliding*, Ol' Diz had a ready, albeit confusing, explanation. "As for saying, 'Rizzuto slud into second,' it just ain't natural. Sounds silly to me. *Slud* is something more than *slid*. It means sliding with great effort."

Clearly logic was also missing from Dizzy's strengths. "It puzzles me how they know what corners are good for filling stations," he once mused aloud. "Just how did they know gas and oil was under there?" Ever faithful to a sponsor, Dean explained his breakfast habits. "Sure I eat Wheaties for breakfast. A good bowl of Wheaties with bourbon can't be beat."

Dean died in Reno, Nevada, in 1974. He was 64. "The good Lord was good to me," the dumb-like-a-fox Dean once said in summary of his life. "He gave me a strong body, a good right arm, and a weak mind."

Leo the Lion

Though far more famous as a manager, Leo Durocher broke in with the Ruth-Gehrig Yankees, moved to Cincinnati, and then became shortstop for the Cardinals in 1933. His take-no-prisoners, "I come to kill you" approach was perfect for the Gashouse Gang. "If I were playing third base and my mother was rounding third with the run that was going to beat us, I would trip her," bragged Durocher. A banjo hitter, though a slick fielder, the 5'10", 160-pound Durocher was named to three All-Star squads—one in 1936 for St. Louis—in a playing career that lasted until 1945.

Durocher left the Cardinals and became player/manager in Brooklyn in 1939. By 1946 Durocher had managed winning Dodgers teams in seven of his first eight big-league seasons and won a pennant. Exiled from baseball in the 1947 season for gambling and fired by the Dodgers in midseason the following year, Durocher immediately moved across town to lead the hated New York Giants, where in seven full campaigns he turned in five more winning seasons, two pennants, and a World Series title. A decade later he rebuilt the Chicago Cubs and then finished his career in Houston with the Astros in 1973.

Born in West Springfield, Massachusetts, on July 27, 1905, Durocher was the classic little-man underdog battling his way through life under the cover of a false daring and confidence. He started as an altar boy at St. Louis de France Church and finished with a spiritual awakening in his closing years in Palm Springs, California, where he returned to the church and sincerely sought spiritual counsel to overcome a lifelong habit of swearing. In between, his life was not so healthy.

Claiming to be so poor that he "never had a Christmas tree," Leo was into pool hustling in his teens. He would borrow several dollars

TRIVIA

What did Branch Rickey say Durocher had a special capacity for doing when in a bad situation?

Answers to the trivia questions are on pages 161–162.

and run his winnings upward to pay off the debt, only to lose in an impulsive desire for continued action. There is no record of Durocher ever attending high school.

His gambling addiction took many forms: pool hustling, dice rolling, card playing, horse racing, and possibly baseball betting. In his sixties, Durocher was investigated for gambling by Commissioner Bowie Kuhn. He made a career of keeping company with unsavory characters, a practice that earned him the yearlong suspension in 1947 and was likely the reason the FBI kept a file on him.

Durocher loved life on the edge. His pockets were constantly empty despite hefty salaries, as Durocher ran up gambling debts and borrowed money to pay them off and keep in the action. Adventurous sex was another apparent high for Leo, who boasted about his conquests. Openly adulterous throughout his marriages, he was charged by Ray Hendricks as a corespondent in Hendricks' divorce from Laraine Day. In 1964 a Middlebury, Vermont, man charged Leo—then 58—with alienation of affection, claiming Durocher had stolen his wife while dating the man's 26-year-old daughter. Well into his sixties, the newly married Durocher reportedly took up with a Montreal usherette for a one-night stand. Approaching 72 and living with a woman approximately 40 years his junior, Leo had a penile implant to sustain his sexual performance.

Risk-taking and action-seeking led to brawling, frequent fines, and suspensions. Durocher was charged by fans with assault and battery on three occasions. Durocher accounted for his impulsivity by claiming the cardinal tenet by which he lived was "If you feel like doing it, do it, and it will all come out right in the end."

Durocher feuded with media figures he didn't like, infuriating beat writers with insults, refusals to talk, and lies about who his starter on a given day might be. "I felt he went out of his way to slight me and the rest

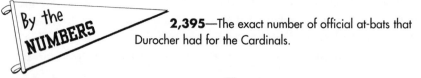

2,395—The exact number of official at-bats that Durocher had for the Cardinals.

More famous as a manager than a player, Leo Durocher was a scrappy member of the Gashouse Gang, playing a sterling shortstop for the Cardinals from 1933 to 1937.

of the broadcasters and sportswriters who covered his exploits daily," noted famed Chicago announcer Jack Brickhouse.

That Durocher almost never spoke about his childhood suggested the experience was one of emotional deprivation rather than pool-hustling glories. He concealed his insecurities under a façade of braggadocio, ever retelling events in self-congratulatory ways or spinning clearly false, self-glorifying tales. Legendary baseball columnist Jerome Holtzman labeled Durocher a pathological liar. Hall of Fame umpire Jocko Conlan said, "He could have been one of the all-time greats. My gripe with Leo is that he just wasn't truthful."

And the little man from West Springfield had to be the center of attention. Writer Tom Meany tells of Leo's first spring training trip in 1926 as a Yankees prospect. The flashily clad Durocher took a seat in the veterans' poker game aboard a Pullman train car.

"What's the name, keed?" queried the Babe himself.

"Leo Durocher," the 20-year-old replied.

"It was our first introduction to this rookie shortstop," Meany recounted later, "but so help me, Durocher wasn't in that poker game more than five minutes before he was telling the Babe how to run it."

Possessing a raspy voice and cold blue eyes, Leo had a thirst for elegance, luxuriating in wearing expensive, tightly tailored suits. He placed his baseball cap on a hat blocker so he would "look professional." Said Cubs traveling secretary Blake Cullen, "He dressed like a million bucks. He was the only guy I ever knew who carried spare teeth. He had these two false front teeth, and he always carried two spares in this little jeweled cuff-link box, just in case somebody took a swing at him and knocked out his teeth."

TRIVIA

For which quote is Durocher most famous?

Answers to the trivia questions are on pages 161–162.

Durocher also sought attention by dropping names. He regularly referred to his friend Frank, although few can recall Sinatra ever reciprocating. Beyond Sinatra, Durocher made certain all in earshot knew he lived with then-famous actor George Raft during one of his early but not infrequent baseball sabbaticals.

His in-your-face verbal style earned him the moniker "the Lip," and his feuds and confrontations with umpires are a part of baseball lore. In one instance, George Magerkurth, a hulking umpire, got into it with Durocher, and in his zeal to make a point, he inadvertently splattered some tobacco juice on Leo.

Durocher spit back.

"That'll cost you, Durocher. You spit on me," asserted Magerkurth.

"What do you think this is all over my face," bellowed Durocher, "smallpox?"

"My spitting was an accident," the umpire stated firmly.

"Mine wasn't," barked Leo, ever getting the edge.

In another imbroglio, the skipper roared out of the dugout to confront the great Beans Reardon over a tight call, and while deliberately kicking lime on Reardon's pants, Durocher demanded, "Was that ball fair or foul?"

"I guess it was a fair ball," answered the umpire.

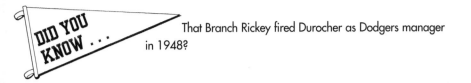

That Branch Rickey fired Durocher as Dodgers manager in 1948?

"You guess? You guess!" barked Durocher. He then strutted away mouthing some uncomplimentary remarks about Reardon's ancestry.

Taking the bait, Beans chased after Leo and challenged, "Just what's that you called me?"

The Lip then sprung the trap, replying in a condescendingly sweet tone, "Well, guess what I called you, Beans. You've spent the whole afternoon guessing at everything else."

Durocher's insecurities made him a user, and even abuser, of others. When he was a manager, myriad players had the experience of being lauded by Leo at one point, only to be discarded like yesterday's newspaper later on. "What have you done for me lately?" could easily have been his epitaph.

In a precomputer, prestatistical era, no one had a better feel for the flow of a baseball game, and his street smarts as well as his unwillingness to yield the PR throne to anyone, served Leo well in keeping his players in line. He had an uncanny nose for talent, identifying Willie Mays and Jackie Robinson as upcoming stars early on. With Robinson, he openly resisted the prevailing racism of the day and supported Branch Rickey's Great Experiment. Later, in retooling the Cubs, Durocher had the ability to sniff out young talent and the resourcefulness to deploy it effectively.

TRIVIA

Leo Durocher made it into the Hall of Fame as a manager. Did he ever manage the Cardinals?

Answers to the trivia questions are on pages 161–162.

The charismatic Durocher could charm and inspire or ride and drive when he wanted to, instilling enthusiasm and pulling extra effort out of players. He was also decisive and well-practiced at projecting an assured persona. He loved to manage, with the dugout his comfort zone—the one place in which his image as a successful leader was early and firmly established.

Other Members of the 1934 Gang

Pepper Martin was a maverick. "He was a bundle of energy," noted writer Fred Lieb, "couldn't sit still for a minute, and was unpredictable." Martin hitch-hiked to his first spring training in 1928 and continued his daring ways by riding railroads (an illegal practice at the time). He was once arrested in Georgia and spent an evening enjoying the accommodations afforded by the Thomasville city jail. The following day he reported to the Redbirds with an unkempt beard, dirty clothes, and his face adorned with oil and grease.

After becoming a star for St. Louis, where he played his entire 13-year career, he continued to look like an unmade bed with dirty sheets. He enjoyed midget auto racing and would spend his mornings working on cars, arriving just in time for batting practice and looking the part of an unwashed mechanic.

A lifetime .298 hitter, the four-time All-Star's greatest asset was his blinding speed. He led the league in stolen bases three times and finished second once.

Martin was highly superstitious and believed that hairpins generated good fortune—a longstanding belief among many players. In Cincinnati Roy Stockton and Ray Gillespie, a pair of writers, decided to scatter a bag of hairpins around the hotel lobby, expecting to be amused by Martin's pursuit of them. Joe Medwick, however, got there first and began collecting them.

"Hey, those are for Pepper Martin," Stockton stated.

"Let Pepper find his own hairpins," Medwick replied, and then walked off with the good-luck tokens in his pockets. Ducky Medwick was combative and unpopular, constantly involved in fights. "Ducky" is actually the shortened version of "Ducky Wucky," a tag placed on Medwick in 1931 when he played in Houston. Not surprisingly, Medwick detested the moniker— short or long—and preferred to be called Mickey, a childhood tag derived

Pepper Martin was probably the ringleader of the Gashouse Gang, the Cardinals' famed group of characters who made up the core of its thirties powerhouse. The third baseman/outfielder spent 13 seasons with the Cardinals.

DID YOU KNOW . . . That Bill Hallahan looked forward to the first ever All-Star Game, particularly to seeing Babe Ruth? "We wanted to see the Babe," Hallahan recalled. "Sure he was old and had a big waistline, but that didn't make any difference. We were on the same field as Babe Ruth." Indeed Hallahan was. He was the starting pitcher for the NL that day. He was also the losing pitcher, yielding a home run to—you guessed it—the 38-year-old Ruth in the third inning. It was Hallahan's only All-Star Game.

from his middle name, Michael. His teammates sometimes called him "Muscles" because of his physique.

Disagreeable as he was, Medwick was a great—Hall of Fame—player. Despite a .319 average and his 106 RBIs in 1934, the bad-ball-hitting Medwick was still three years away from his greatest season, 1937, when he took the last NL Triple Crown.

Ripper Collins was a party animal for the rabble-rousing Gashouse Gang. "Rickey always accused me of being the ringleader," said Collins. "I never could understand why he picked on me—unless it could have been because there was considerable truth in the allegations." Trapped in the minors for a long time, Collins managed only three or four solid seasons, but few offensive players were his superior in 1934, when he swatted 35 home runs and drove home 128 to go with a .333 mark.

Paul Dean was nicknamed "Daffy," but the label was hardly accurate, rather an alliterative counterpart to his older brother's "Dizzy." The younger Dean was serious and shy, very unlike Ol' Diz, who had this to say after Paul's no-hitter: "I wished I'da known Paul was goin' to pitch a no-hitter. I'da pitched one, too." Paul had a strong rookie season in 1934, posting 19 victories. More important, he won two Series outings with an ERA of just 1.00. Paul won 19 again in 1935. Given the indications of his eventual greatness, the 22-year-old held out for more money going into the next season. Once signed, he hurried back, injured his arm, and was never the same. He went just 5–5 in 1936 and won only seven more major league games after that.

TRIVIA

The Dean brothers were one and two in wins, notching 49 of the Cardinals' 95 victories in 1934. Who was third in wins?

Answers to the trivia questions are on pages 161–162.

Any member of the 1934 Cardinals with the nickname "Wild Bill" figures to be quite a story. In the case of Bill Hallahan, however, the reader will be disappointed. The left-hander got this tag for his propensity to walk batters. And walk them he did, leading the league in bases on balls distributed in 1930, 1931,

TRIVIA

What memorable incident occurred in Medwick's life when he was with the Dodgers in 1940?

Answers to the trivia questions are on pages 161–162.

and 1933. Moreover, he led the league in wild pitches three times. Hallahan was hard to hit, however. He led the league in whiffs in 1930 and 1931. Wild Bill, though not a big man at 5'10½", 170 pounds, was a mainstay in the Cardinals rotation for six years, beginning in 1930. He went 85–58 from 1930 to 1935, starting 163 games and completing 76. He won 19 in 1931. Curiously, 1934 was an off year for the aging Hallahan—who turned 32 that August—going just 8–12 with a 4.26 ERA.

Hallahan was a clutch big-game pitcher. He appeared in seven World Series games and started five. Not only was he 3–1 in those encounters, but he also turned in a microscopic 1.36 ERA over 40 innings of work, extraordinary for a pitcher whose lifetime ERA was 4.03.

Spud Davis, an estimable performer who hit .300 in 10 of his 16 seasons, often caught for Hallahan. He was a lead-footed receiver with not much of an arm, but he could sear those line drives and finished with a .308 average in 1,458 contests. In the special 1934 season, Davis hit an even .300 in 347 at-bats.

Amid the joy there was also tragedy. Davis shared catching duties with Bill DeLancey, an effective backstop who could hit left-handed. He broke into the majors in 1932 when he was 20. DeLancey had great promise, particularly in the eyes of Branch Rickey, who placed the backstop on his all-time team even though he appeared in only 219 major league games. In 1934 DeLancey platooned with Spud Davis, hitting .316, driving in 40 runs, and swatting 13 round-trippers in just 253 at-bats. The next year he slumped, appearing tired. At season's end he was diagnosed with tuberculosis. He then missed four years before trying unsuccessfully to come back in 1940. He died on his 35th birthday on November 28, 1946.

No Cigars

Often fans fail to appreciate a championship team or era sufficiently, believing that somehow the victory beat will go on in perpetuity. Cardinals fans had, on one hand, every reason to believe the Gashouse Gang would continue to play championship-level baseball. After all, Frisch, Martin, Durocher, Collins, and Medwick were all back on the field, while the Dean brothers, along with Wild Bill Hallahan and Bill Walker, returned to the mound. On the other hand, there were reasons for concern. Although the Dean pair and Medwick were still in their twenties, the rest were east of thirty—a real boundary in a heavy-drinking, short-lifespan, pre–sports medicine and nutrition era. Frisch, the leader, was an ancient 36. Besides, despite the champagne season of 1934, the next year the team had to come roaring down the stretch to finish ahead of Bill Terry's Giants in the NL.

So how did things turn out? Frisch's squad delivered another strong season in 1935, going 96–58, a half game better than the 1934 club. The team scored 30 more runs than the previous season (829), many of those on the strength of upcoming superstar Joe Medwick, who placed in the top four in nine offensive categories, hitting .353 and driving in 126 runs. The Deans rang up 47 victories, while the two Bills—Hallahan and Walker—added 28 more. Charlie Grimm's Cubs, however, put up 100 wins and took the title.

It was a bitter pill, but Redbirds backers could take comfort in knowing they were rooting for a truly winning organization, one still operated by Breadon and Rickey. Things, however, were not the same in 1936, as the team won 87 and dropped 67, a 9-game slide from 1935. What made it particularly frustrating was that the Giants copped the flag with only 92 triumphs. Age had begun creeping up by 1936: Frisch was a part-time player, and the Hallahan-Walker duo was rendered impotent, with the former shipped to Cincinnati and the latter contributing just five victories. Even worse, Paul Dean dropped from two straight 19-game seasons to a 5–5 campaign, although brother Diz pressed on with a 24–13 season.

TRIVIA

How did Lon Warneke stay in the game after his pitching career was over?

Answers to the trivia questions are on pages 161–162.

The following season was the year of Joe Medwick. Although the team slipped to a fourth-place 81–73 mark, Ducky—as he hated to be called—hit .374, hammered 31 homers, and knocked in a mind-numbing 154 runs to win the Triple Crown, something no National Leaguer managed to do for the rest of the 20th century. The 1937 season was also the one in which Dizzy Dean was injured in the All-Star Game, turning what looked like a 25-win season into a modest 13–10 year. Another 1937 highlight was Lon Warneke, a tremendous pitcher. More than just a fastball pitcher, he had the whole arsenal. By 1932, at just 23, Lon had become one of the absolute best pitchers in baseball, going 22–6 with a 2.32 ERA for the Cubs. His win total and ERA topped the NL. By the end of 1936, Warneke had already won 100 games (losing just 59). He was only 27. In 1937, when he went to St. Louis, he posted 83 more victories against 49 losses over the next five and a half seasons. Washed up at the then old-for-baseball age of 33, Warneke returned to the Cubs, going just 10–13 until his retirement in 1945.

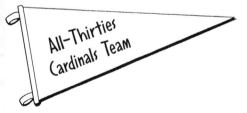

All-Thirties Cardinals Team

Position	Player
First Base	Johnny Mize
Second Base	Frankie Frisch
Third Base	Pepper Martin
Shortstop	Leo Durocher
Left Field	Joe Medwick
Center Field	Terry Moore
Right Field	George Watkins
Pitcher	Dizzy Dean
Catcher	Jimmie Wilson
Manager	Frankie Frisch

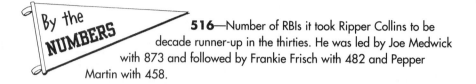

516—Number of RBIs it took Ripper Collins to be decade runner-up in the thirties. He was led by Joe Medwick with 873 and followed by Frankie Frisch with 482 and Pepper Martin with 458.

One wonders whether Warneke might have reached Hall of Fame heights had he been a bit less droll and lazy, because he was right behind Dizzy Dean in pitching effectiveness during Dean's heyday. He was also right behind Dean in character. Though less self-promoting than Dean, Warneke was another hillbilly who loved a good time. He embraced nightlife and humor. According to Bill James, the 19-year-old was better known for messing with snakes than for pitching well in the Cotton States minor league in 1928. When a flat tire stalled the team bus Warneke reportedly waded into a nearby swamp, seized a serpent, and "cracked the whip" with it. He was once ejected from a game for pirating snakes into the dugout.

He was also fond of haberdasheries and was renowned for buying suits when he was a rookie with the Cubs. When the team wanted him to consult a physician in 1932, Warneke refused on peculiar grounds. He had never been to a doctor before and wasn't going to start then. Though far quieter than Dean, Warneke—like Ol' Diz—was full of folk wisdom.

He was also a musician and carried a ukulele with him regularly to play in the clubhouse. It was more than a prank to Warneke, as he played in Pepper Martin's Mudcat Band in the thirties and forties. It was from his musical orientation rather than his fastball that he acquired the nickname "the Arkansas Hummingbird."

Unfortunately, by 1938 the fans could declare the Gashouse Era officially over. Frisch was out

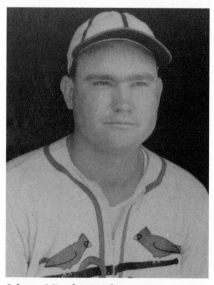

Johnny Mize hit 218 home runs as a Cardinal from 1936 to 1941.

as manager late in the season, Durocher was a Dodger, Dizzy Dean a Cub (joining Ripper Collins who had been dispatched to Chicago in 1937), and Pepper Martin and Paul Dean were nonfactors. Only Joe Medwick continued to be a force, coming up with a .322 average backed by 122 RBIs and 21 homers. Young Johnny Mize, then in his third season, added 27 homers and 102 RBIs, as he started building what would become Hall of Fame credentials.

A revamped Cardinals team closed the decade on a high note, winning 92 of 153 decisions and finishing second to the Reds under new skipper Ray Blades. Mize, Medwick, Terry Moore, and Enos Slaughter drove the offense, with Medwick as their leader for the decade, hitting 145 homers and driving in 873 runs. Curt Davis went 22–16 in front of a balanced pitching staff, one that had six hurlers win at least 10 games.

Although the team won 427 of 766 decisions from 1935 through 1939, there were no cigars to go with three second-place finishes.

The Cardinals began establishing themselves in the twenties, when they managed an 822–712 decade mark to go with two pennants and one World Series title. The Cardinals became a genuine force, however, by the end of the thirties. That decade saw the team win 869 games, while losing 665—204 games over .500—for a .566 winning percentage. There were three pennants and three more second-place finishes to go with their 1934 World Series championship. Little did Redbirds fans know what lay in the decade just ahead.

DID YOU KNOW . . . That the Cardinals had eight winning seasons in both the twenties and the thirties?

The Early Forties

The big news in 1940 was that the Cardinals, after much wrangling, were able to reach an agreement with the Browns to split the $150,000 cost of installing lights in Sportsman's Park. The Browns hosted the first night game on May 24, while the Cardinals played in artificial lighting for the first time on June 4, when they fell to the Brooklyn Dodgers by a lopsided 10–1, despite Joe Medwick's going 5 for 5. For the season, the Cardinals took an eight-game slide from 1939, going 84–69 in their second year under Ray Blades, although the lead-footed, red-faced slugger Johnny Mize whacked 43 homers.

Rickey, however, was obviously troubled by the team's performance, as Blades was relieved of his duties when the Cards stumbled out of the gate at 14–24. Mike Gonzalez held the reins for six games, winning just once. Billy Southworth then returned after an 11-year sabbatical as Cardinals skipper, making him the Cardinals multiterm manager with the longest period of time between tours of duty.

The 1941 Cardinals managed a 97–56 record under Southworth, a record that fell a maddening two and a half games shy of the Dodgers' 100–54 mark. Highlights of the season included a no-hitter by Lon Warneke on August 30 and another by Hank Gornicki, who in his major league debut on May 3 fired a one-hitter in a 6–0 triumph over Philadelphia. The St. Louis euphoria over Gornicki was short-lived, however, as the masterpiece was his only win as a Cardinal and one of only 15 in his major league career.

On December 7, 1941, the Japanese bombed Hawaii's Pearl Harbor, and the United States went to war. Commissioner Landis considered shutting down the game, but as spring training approached, he wrote President Franklin Roosevelt asking for counsel as to whether to go

Billy Southworth, shown here with New York Giants manager John McGraw, managed the Cardinals to five straight seasons with 90-plus wins during the forties, including championships in 1942 and 1944.

forward with a season. Roosevelt responded with the "Green Light Letter." Believing that baseball contributed favorably to the morale of the nation, FDR wrote, "I honestly feel it would be best for the country to keep baseball going." The commissioner's response was gracious. "I hope that our performance will be such as to justify the president's faith," stated baseball's autocratic czar.

The following season St. Louis turned in a 106–48 season under Southworth. The team won an astounding 60 games at Sportsman's Park. With Mize gone to New York, the Cardinals featured shortstop Marty Marion, third baseman Whitey Kurowski, outfielders Terry Moore and

Enos Slaughter, and a rookie named Stan Musial, who hit .315 and 10 homers. Mort Cooper won 22 games against just seven defeats and registered a phenomenal 1.78 ERA, good enough for NL MVP. One-year wonder Johnny Beazley went 21–6 with a runner-up 2.13 ERA. The Nashville, Tennessee, native won only 10 other big-league games.

TRIVIA

Johnny Mize set a major league record for hitting three home runs in a single game. How many times did he do it?

Answers to the trivia questions are on pages 161–162.

After losing the Series opener to the Yankees, the Cardinals stormed to four straight wins to take the championship. Champagne flowed in the city of blues, as the Cardinals claimed their fourth world title. Amid the good times, however, there was a sour note. Branch Rickey was driven out of St. Louis by office politics, and he headed to Brooklyn to take control of the Dodgers.

DID YOU KNOW . . . That on April 23, 1940, a flood at Cincinnati's Crosley Field washed out a game between the Redbirds and the Reds, the first time ever a game was postponed due to a flood? The teams decided to make up the game on May 13, when the two teams would both head east. There was one oversight, however. The teams failed to alert the NL office of the makeup date, and therefore there were no umpires. Cincinnati coach Jimmy Wilson and ace pitcher Lon Warneke were pressed into service before Larry Goetz, an umpire who resided in Cincinnati, forfeited his day off and came to arbitrate the game. Still, the April 23 game was not truly made up, as the May 13 contest ended in an 8–8 tie after 14 innings.

The War Years

By 1943 Branch Rickey was gone and World War II was on in full force. Baseball was greatly affected by the military conflict, as a host of its greatest players headed off to serve Uncle Sam. Hank Greenberg, Joe DiMaggio, Bob Feller, and Ted Williams spent time away from the game during the war years. With the United States fully engaged in military combat, Cubs owner and gum magnate P. K. Wrigley received word from President Roosevelt that major league baseball may have to be suspended due to a manpower shortage. Wrigley, wanting to ensure that the game remained alive until the men returned, joined with Rickey to start the first women's professional league. Adopting rules from the men's game, the new game was faster than softball. The athletes—required to attend charm school—were expected to express a contemporary femininity and adhere to a strict code of conduct. The league lasted from 1943 through 1954 with seasons running from 110 to 120 games in length. In 1948 the 10-team league drew 910,000 fans.

The tragic downside of this ingenious experiment was that African Americans continued to be left out. As minimally skilled white players dotted major league rosters and the women's game was created, stellar African-American players remained banished from the game, a position Commissioner Landis steadfastly maintained.

During this time, the Cardinals, without star outfielder Enos Slaughter, repeated as NL champs with a 105–49 record under then highly successful manager Billy Southworth. They won the NL flag by 18 games over Cincinnati. Young Stan Musial became all the rage in 1943, leading the league in average (.357), hits (220), doubles (48), triples (20), total bases (347), and slugging percentage (.562). Despite these powerful numbers he hit just 13 home runs.

The 1944 season featured the only all–St Louis World Series in history and the lone appearance of the American League's St. Louis Browns in the fall classic.

The team's primary success was its pitching, as Redbirds hurlers compiled a team ERA of just 2.57, far and away the best in a league that had an ERA average of 3.37. The Cardinals staff threw 21 shutouts, and the team allowed just 475 runs all season, barely three runs per game. Mort Cooper went 21–8 with a 2.30 ERA, and Max Lanier was 15–7 with a 1.90 ERA.

The Series was a Yankees-Cardinals rematch. The Redbirds once again dropped the opener but came back to win the second game. That, however, is where similarities ended, as the men from the Bronx swept the next three games and the World Series title.

By 1944 the Cardinals had the look of a dynasty, as the team roared to another 105–49 season and its third straight NL title. Pitching ruled again in 1944—Cooper, Lanier, Ted Wilks, and Harry Brecheen combined for 72 wins in 100 decisions, and the team posted another sparkling 2.67 ERA. The Cardinals also copped their third straight MVP. This time ace shortstop Marty Marion took the honor. Their World Series opponents in 1944 would be none other than their fellow Sportsman's Park tenants, the St. Louis Browns, who won their first—and last, as it turned out—AL pennant. It was called the "streetcar series" because that was the prevailing mode of urban travel in St. Louis at the time.

TRIVIA

What happened with the 1945 All-Star Game?

Answers to the trivia questions are on pages 161–162.

To say that pitching dominated the 1944 all–St. Louis World Series would be an understatement. The two teams combined for only 28 runs in six games, and the ERAs for the Cardinals and Browns were 1.96 and 1.49, respectively. The teams barely topped the .200 mark in hitting with only 85 hits in 403 at-bats. The Series also turned on defense, as the Browns committed ten errors against just one by the Cardinals. The lone Redbirds miscue was committed by Stan Musial, who managed to hit .304 despite the mound dominance.

The Series lacked for little when it came to excitement. The Browns took the lead 2–1, opening with nine-game winner Denny Galehouse besting the estimable Mort Cooper. Another one-run nail-biter followed, going to the Redbirds. Things began looking grim for the National Leaguers when the Browns took a 6–2 contest in Game 3. From there, however, it was all Cardinals pitching. The Series turned largely on Harry Brecheen's stellar performance in Game 4. Brecheen, who went 16–5 during the regular season, squared the Series at two each. The Redbirds won Games 4, 5, and 6, 5–1, 2–0, and 3–1, respectively, and had their third-straight pennant.

DID YOU KNOW . . . That Red Barrett and Ken Burkhart, who combined for 40 Cardinals wins in 1945, did not together win even 100 major league games? Charles "Red" Barrett finished his career 69–69, while Burkhart went 28–20.

TRIVIA

What effect did the war have on major league attendance?

Answers to the trivia questions are on pages 161–162.

Could the Cardinals win four straight pennants? Maybe even another World Series? Could they do it without the great, then-24-year-old Stan Musial? Those were the questions in the minds of Redbirds fans as the 1945 campaign approached. The team still had Marty Marion and Whitey Kurowski, and it added a young newcomer named Al "Red" Schoendienst to the field, but only Brecheen and Wilks returned among the star moundsmen.

Behind the pitching of the killer B's, Red Barrett and Ken Burkhart, who went a combined 39–17 for the team, the Cardinals put together a 95–59 championship-level season. Unfortunately, Charlie Grimm's Cubs were three games better, so the pennant streak ended at three. For manager Billy Southworth, the near-miss was only a minor disappointment, as his son, Billy Southworth Jr., the first player in organized baseball to enlist in the military during World War II, died when his B-29 crashed off the coast of Flushing, New York, on February 15, just before the season began.

The Man

Stanley Frank Musial may well be the most underpublicized of all of the great game's all-time greats. First, although he is called "the Man," there was nothing physically imposing about Musial. He stood just 5'10" and weighed 175 pounds, the physique of an undersized short-stop in the modern game. Second, and perhaps more important, Musial generated absolutely no stimulating press. He was not flamboyant like Babe Ruth, flashy like Willie Mays, controversial like Ted Williams, nasty like Ty Cobb, or difficult like Barry Bonds. Stan Musial was pure class. "An exact opposite of Williams," wrote Roger Kahn, "the perfect gentleman, the perfect sport. Never angry at draft boards, seldom spits in public, always hits with enthusiasm, smiles often. Successful without arrogance, he represents the milder side of those who admire him."

Musial's roots were very ordinary. He was born on November 21, 1920, in Donora, Pennsylvania, the first son and second youngest of six children. His mother was Czech and his father a Polish immigrant who labored in the local mines. Stan (a shortened version of Stanislaus) was a standout early in both baseball and basketball.

Life was hard in the mines and steel mills of Pennsylvania, and his father, Lukasz, understandably wanted young Stan to use a college education as a way to escape from the blue-collar existence. Young Musial, however, was a C– student and was offered a minor league contract at a young age. Stan wept when his father refused to sign it. His mother then intervened and convinced Lukasz to let their son pursue his dream.

For 17-year-old Stan it was not about hitting, it was about pitching. And he was good. By 1940, in his third year in the Cardinals system, he had an 18–5 record and had compiled a lifetime 33–13 win-loss mark.

By the NUMBERS

25—Number of truly astonishing accomplishments in Stan Musial's career that are listed below:

- He was consistent.
- Finishing his career with an incredible 3,630 hits, Musial compiled 1,815 at home and the same number on the road.
- He scored 1,949 runs and drove in 1,951.
- He hit .310 or better for 16 straight seasons, finishing with a lifetime average of .331.
- He averaged better than 200 hits per season between ages 22 and 35.
- Just short of his 42nd birthday he turned in a .330 season.
- He scored more than 100 runs 11 times.
- He drove in more than 100 runs 10 times.
- He hit more than 20 home runs 10 times, finishing with 475.
- He hit 30 or more doubles 16 times, finishing with 725.
- He hit 10 or more triples eight times, finishing with 177.
- He was on the All-Star team 20 times.
- He missed the 1948 Triple Crown by one homer, batting .376, driving in 131 runs, and belting 39 homers.
- He was the first player in major league history to win three MVP awards.
- He hit a record five home runs in a doubleheader.
- He won seven batting titles.
- He led the NL in on-base percentage six times.
- He led the NL in slugging six times.
- He led the league in games played five times.
- He led the league in runs five times.
- He led the league in hits six times.
- He led the league in total bases six times.
- He led the league in doubles eight times.
- He led the league in triples five times.
- He led the league in extra-base hits seven times.

That August Musial severely injured his shoulder while playing the outfield, something he did when not pitching (because teams had small rosters and Musial had already proven his hitting prowess). He never regained sufficient arm strength to pitch again. "I couldn't throw hard from then," recalls Musial. "It never bothered my hitting. Even if I didn't hurt my arm, I think somewhere along the line, somebody would have

Stan "the Man" Musial played in 895 consecutive games, was the first Cardinal to collect 3,000 career hits, and is generally considered one of the 10 greatest outfielders of all time.

TRIVIA

Where does the Cardinals' 1942 106–48 record rank in team history?

Answers to the trivia questions are on pages 161–162.

switched me over to an outfielder anyway, because my hitting was always good."

Perhaps Musial was correct, because the scouting report on his pitching after his first two years recommended his release. He was wild and inconsistent despite his then 15–8 record. Nonetheless, this look-at-the-bright-side attitude typified Musial. "Like Mays, he saw the world entirely in terms of his own good fortune," wrote Curt Flood. "He was convinced it was the best of all possible worlds. He not only accepted baseball mythology but propounded it. Gibson and I once clocked eight *wunner-fuls* in a Musial speech that could not have been more than 100 words."

In 1941 Musial was transformed from a weak-armed outfielder playing at the Class C level into a dynamo in the International League, and he went on to become a late-season addition to the team's major league roster. Musial made his mark instantly, collecting an amazing 20 hits in 47 trips against major league pitchers. The Cardinals were sold, and he became a fixture in the Redbirds lineup beginning in 1942, except in 1945 when he served in the navy during the war. Star that he was, Musial fit in as a Cardinal quickly and well. "Stan was a good ol' country boy," said the great Marty Marion. "No, if you didn't like Stan, you don't like anybody."

A lefty all the way, the only thing unorthodox about Musial was his batting stance. He stood in a crouch, with his body twisted such that his back all but faced the pitcher. Then when the pitch was on its way, he would uncoil, pushing off his left leg for maximum power in his long stride, and sear the bat through the strike zone with near-miraculous results.

Ironically he did not get his nickname from anyone related to the Cardinals. It happened in Brooklyn's Ebbets Field in 1946, when Dodger-killer Musial made his way to the plate and a Flatbush fan lamented, "Uh-oh, here comes the man again. Here comes the man."

Bob Costas summarized Musial brilliantly in a feature on the Man on ESPN's *SportsCentury*: "He didn't hit a homer in his last at-bat; he hit a single. He didn't hit in 56 straight games. He married his high school sweetheart and stayed married to her, never married a Marilyn Monroe. He didn't play with the sheer joy and style that goes alongside Willie Mays' name. None of those easy things are there to associate with Stan Musial. All Musial represents is more than two decades of sustained excellence and complete decency as a human being."

There stands outside Busch Stadium a 10-foot statue of the Man. It has been there since 1968. The inscription is a quote from Commissioner Ford Frick upon Musial's retirement: "Here stands baseball's perfect warrior. Here stands baseball's perfect knight."

Back to Normal

In 1946, with the war in the rearview mirror, baseball was back to normal. The 1946 season figured to be a sweet one for Cardinals fans, as the team would be at full strength for the NL race. Branch Rickey, however, had things moving in Brooklyn with Leo Durocher at the throttle. The two teams battled it out so evenly that the season ended with each having won 96 games against 58 losses. The Cardinals, under new skipper Eddie Dyer, swept the best-of-three playoff two games to nothing and went on to play the Boston Red Sox in the World Series. It was one battle royal, with the Series coming down to a seventh and final game in St. Louis. With the score tied at three in the eighth, one of the great moments in Cardinals history occurred. Harry Walker doubled to left-center and Enos "Country" Slaughter took off in what was called the "mad dash," scoring from first to give the Redbirds the winning run.

It was typical Slaughter. "He's a little old, but he'll pinch hit any time for you," said Casey Stengel in Stengelese, "and even if it weren't for nothing else, he's got the spirit that makes a ballclub go like you'll hardly ever see." Slaughter, known for his hustle, was a Gold Glove–level outfielder in an era before such awards were granted. His hustle made him immensely popular among Cardinals fans, despite his rather grouchy personality. Slaughter later smudged his reputation by being part of a group of 1947 Dodgers who threatened to strike if Jackie Robinson was allowed to play on their team. The rebellion was quickly quelled by NL president Ford Frick, who promised suspensions for any offending player.

Slaughter made it into the Hall of Fame in 1985, long after his eligibility began, and, typical of Slaughter, he complained. "I think with my record, I deserved to be in there at least 10 to 15 years before I went in," he grumbled in 1994. "A lot of guys went through that era, but I hit better than they did. They went in and never did get to .300. I think when you stay in the big leagues and hit .300, I think you need consideration." Some feel Slaughter's alleged resistance to Robinson, plus his involvement in a spiking of Robinson, held back his entrance to the Hall. Slaughter vehemently denied being party to any planned strike involving Robinson and claimed the spiking was an accident. At least Slaughter lived to see his induction, as Country did not die until 2002, at age 86.

Enos "Country" Slaughter scored the winning run of Game 7 of the 1946 World Series in dramatic fashion, coming around from first on a Harry Walker double in the eighth inning.

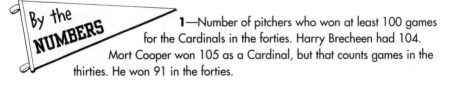

All-Forties Cardinals Team

Position	Player
First Base	Johnny Hopp
Second Base	Red Schoendienst
Third Base	Whitey Kurowski
Shortstop	Marty Marion
Left Field	Stan Musial
Center Field	Terry Moore
Right Field	Enos Slaughter
Pitcher	Harry Brecheen
Catcher	Walker Cooper
Manager	Billy Southworth

Hopp gets the nod over Ray Sanders at first, and Brecheen edges out Mort Cooper, because the Sanders and Cooper stats may well have been aided by the absence of key players during the war years.

Despite Slaughter's heroics, Harry Brecheen was the Series star, winning three games after saving the clincher over the Dodgers in the NL playoffs. His Series ERA was 0.45. Stan Musial claimed the league MVP award, hitting .365 to lead the league.

Though few expected it at the time, with the close of the 1946 season, the Cardinals' run as a dominant team was over. In 1947, with Jackie Robinson understandably the game's big story, the Cardinals finished five games behind the Dodgers with an 89–65 mark. At the end of the season, longtime Cardinals owner Sam Breadon sold the team to Robert Hannegan and Fred Saigh. In 1948 it was 85–69 and another second-place finish, with Musial again the bright spot, winning his third MVP.

The Cardinals closed the decade coming just a game short in a heart-stopping pennant race with Brooklyn, despite posting a 96–58 record. The team had posted a winning record in ever year of the forties, with the worst, 84–69, coming in 1940. At season's end, Saigh bought out Hannegan to become the Redbirds' sole owner.

By the NUMBERS

1—Number of pitchers who won at least 100 games for the Cardinals in the forties. Harry Brecheen had 104. Mort Cooper won 105 as a Cardinal, but that counts games in the thirties. He won 91 in the forties.

The Ecstasy and the Agony

The team began a noticeable decline in the fifties, failing to win more than 88 games in any of the first four years of the decade. Eddie Dyer was replaced by Marty Marion in 1951, who in turn gave way to Eddie Stanky the following season. In 1952, during a solid 88–66 season, Fred Saigh announced that he would sell the team, and the highest bidders intended to move the team out of St. Louis. The Braves were also moving, from Boston to Milwaukee. Anheuser-Busch, led by its owner, August A. Busch Jr., came to the team's rescue in the 11th hour and kept the club in St. Louis. After the 1953 season, the team bought Sportsman's Park from Browns owner Bill Veeck and renovated and renamed it Busch Stadium in 1954.

On the field, however, Busch was not rewarded, as the team fell to 72–82 by 1954, breaking a 15-year run of winning seasons. Two more losing seasons followed, and the Cardinals were on their way to a disappointing decade, one without a single pennant and just a single, rather distant, second-place finish—to the world champion Milwaukee Braves in 1957, a team aided by a trade at the June deadline for the popular Schoendienst (from the Giants, to whom he was moved during the 1956 season).

Stan Musial was a huge Cardinals newsmaker in the fifties, winning four batting titles and registering his 3,000th hit in Chicago's Wrigley Field on May 13, 1958, while doubling as a pinch-hitter. The 37-year-old hit .337 for the season but would slump to .255 in 1959, the first sub-.300 season of his career. Never a slacker, Musial broke the NL iron man record in 1957 by playing in 895 straight contests before being forced out of the lineup by a torn muscle in his shoulder. Despite the injury, he managed to win the batting title with a .351 mark.

In 1955 the Cardinals brought up a promising 19-year-old bonus baby from Hollis, Oklahoma, named Lindy McDaniel. Given the bonus-baby rules of the time, which required that prize signees be placed on the major league roster immediately, McDaniel went straight to the bigs without tossing a ball in the minor leagues. He debuted on September 2, 1955, and worked 19 innings for the Redbirds that season. The lanky 6'3", 195-pounder had no record but posted a respectable-for-a-19-year-old

Sportsman's Park, home to the Cardinals from 1920 to 1966, became Busch Stadium in 1954, two years after August Busch purchased the Redbirds. It was also the home of the St. Louis Browns from 1902 until their move to Baltimore in 1954.

4.74 ERA. The next year he appeared in 39 games, starting 7 and turning in a 7–6 mark to go with a 3.40 ERA. In 1957 McDaniel, at just 21, made big news by tying for the club lead in wins with 15 (against only nine losses) and completing 10 of his 26 starts while working 191 innings.

Lindy McDaniel was on his way to stardom, and the Cardinals faithful were excited—but not as excited as they were about another Cardinal from Hollis, Oklahoma. Lindy's younger brother Von, just 18, signed as a

7—Number of men who managed the Cardinals in the fifties: Eddie Dyer, Marty Marion, Eddie Stanky, Harry Walker, Fred Hutchinson, Stan Hack, and Solly Hemus.

$50,000 bonus baby. The 6'2", 180-pound younger McDaniel had a smooth, seemingly effortless delivery, one that generated a scintillating fastball and a wicked curve. Like Lindy, Von was a strong Christian. He was also intelligent and sensitive. Von was such a strong player, he didn't even pitch in college, as he simply shook the baseball world by winning his first four major league games. For the season, he started thirteen games and completed four, two of which were shutouts. He pitched 19 scoreless innings and threw a one-hitter, a two-hitter, and a perfect game through six innings. He finished the season 7–5 with a 3.22 ERA.

Yes, Lindy McDaniel was good, but Von was a flat-out phenom—an up-and-coming superstar. Cardinals fans were filled with glee at the pair, believing the two would restore their beloved Redbirds to a perch atop the NL reminiscent of the glorious forties when the McDaniels' forebears, the Dean brothers, dominated the sports headlines. Indeed, the McDaniels, especially Von, were on the lips of baseball fans from coast to coast.

TRIVIA

Gerry Staley led the Cardinals in wins during the fifties with 74 in five seasons. Who was second?

Answers to the trivia questions are on pages 161–162.

In 1958 Lindy struggled to a 5–7 mark, completing just 2 of his 17 starts and turning in a bulging 5.80 ERA. From there the Cardinals decided to make Lindy a reliever, and the rest is a very impressive history, as the elder McDaniel went on to pitch for the Cardinals, Cubs, Giants, Yankees, and Royals in a 21-year career that finally ended in 1975. Lindy made the All-Star team in 1960 and led the league in saves three times. He never pitched in fewer than 54 games from 1959 through 1966, and when he retired, only Hall of Famer Hoyt Wilhelm had pitched in more games than the ordained Church of Christ minister Lindy McDaniel.

So what happened with Von? In reality, nothing happened. Other than two walk-plagued innings in 1958, he never threw another major league pitch. What was the explanation? Did he ruin his arm? In a word, no. His collapse was and is an enduring mystery. Something in his psychological makeup bent him toward baseball tragedy. "He lost his coordination and mechanics," said brother Lindy. "There was no real explanation. Some people thought it was psychological, but who knew about those things then? They sent Von down to the minors, but he couldn't get anyone out. He kept sinking further and further until he couldn't pitch anymore. It depressed him for years after he left baseball, but he couldn't talk about it."

More accurately, McDaniel sunk all the way down to Class D baseball, professional baseball's lowest level. There in the Florida State League of 1960 McDaniel regained his rhythm and fashioned a 13–5 season. The hopeful Cardinals brought him back to spring training the following season, but his magic touch was gone, never to be regained.

Gone prematurely from baseball, Von died in Lawton, Oklahoma, in 1995. He was only 56 years old.

Position	Player
First Base	Stan Musial
Second Base	Red Schoendienst
Third Base	Ken Boyer
Shortstop	Solly Hemus
Left Field	Rip Repulski
Center Field	Wally Moon*
Right Field	Enos Slaughter
Pitcher	Gerry Staley
Catcher	Del Rice
Manager	Eddie Stanky

*Although Moon generally played left or right field, he did play center in 1954. The fifties was a decade in which the Cardinals seemed unable to find a center fielder in whom they had confidence.

Return to Glory

The new decade began auspiciously, as the men under Solly Hemus fought their way to an 86–68 season. The next two campaigns indicated a trailing off (80–74 and 84–78), however, leaving Cardinals fans to wonder if the team might be stuck in low gear—better than .500 but not a contender.

Then came the never-to-be-forgotten 1964 season.

Gene Mauch took over the then-woeful Phillies in 1960 when he was only 34. Mauch never made any secret of his certainty that he was an excellent manager. Who could argue with him? After the Phillies went an ungodly 47–107 in 1961 he drove the team to an 81–80 mark the following season. By 1964 the Phillies figured to be contenders, and they were. With 12 games left in the 1964 season the Philadelphians were 90–60, and 6½ games in the NL lead. The Cardinals seemed destined to fight it out for second place with the Reds and the Giants.

But the Cards were transformed on June 15 when GM Bing Devine made a deal sending pitcher Ernie Broglio to the Chicago Cubs for outfielder Lou Brock. Brock went on to set stolen-base records, get 3,000 hits, and enter the Hall of Fame, resulting in the Brock-for-Broglio being regarded as one of the greatest—if not *the* greatest—baseball heists in history.

That judgment is incredibly unfair. If anything, the deal looked like a whopper favoring the Cubs. In the 28-year-old Broglio, Chicago was getting a pitcher who had one 21-win season and an 18-win campaign the previous season (both times with sub-3.00 ERAs)—this in exchange for an outfielder who in his two seasons as a regular in hitter-friendly Wrigley Field had yet to hit more than .263, smack more than nine homers, score more than 79 runs (often as a leadoff man), get more than

The scoreboard reads:

			NEW YORK	0	0	0	0	0	3	0	0	2	H
30	51		NEW YORK	0	0	0	0	0	3	0	0	2	9
45			ST. LOUIS	0	0	0	3	3	0	1	0		10

OUT
UMPIRES
4 3 5
BASES

GIVE Y
FAIR SH

TO TH
UNITED

The Cardinals won their first championship in 18 years in 1964, closing out the Yankees with a gutsy performance by rising star Bob Gibson (right). Ken Boyer embraces Gibson as Tim McCarver approaches.

35 walks, or drive in more than 37 runs. It was a heist all right, one seemingly pulled by John Holland in the city to the north.

Give Bing Devine credit. He saw what no one else saw in Brock, and Lou Brock delivered, finishing his six-time All-Star career with a .293 average, a then-record 938 stolen bases, 3,023 hits, and 1,610 runs scored.

Still, 1964 looked like another also-ran season, one additionally soured by the August 17 firing of popular GM Bing Devine, in part over the rift that had developed between shortstop Dick Groat and manager Johnny Keane, which owner August Busch got wind of and felt Devine should have prevented. Devine was replaced by Bob Howsam, formerly of the Reds. Devine was liked and respected by the players, uncommon for a GM who negotiated contracts with players in a pre-agent era of low salaries. He did his homework, often sitting on the roof of Busch Stadium during Cardinals games so he could keep up with games and players in other cities on his transistor radio. The players respected this, so they were highly motivated to win in Devine's honor after his unceremonious dismissal.

By the **NUMBERS**

11—Number of players on the 1964 Cardinals team who remained in major sports in some capacity or made sports news after their playing careers were over. They were Bob Gibson, Ken Boyer, Bill White, Tim McCarver, Lou Brock, Mike Shannon, Dal Maxvill, Bob Uecker, Dick Groat, Curt Flood, and Joe Morgan.

They were poised when the Phillies lost 10 straight—the greatest swoon in baseball history.

They were swept by the Reds, then the Braves, and then the Cardinals, who were en route to winning nine straight of their own. The starting pitchers were effective, the hitting kicked in, and, as is so often the case with special seasons, an unexpected contributor emerged. Barney Schultz, a 38-year-old knuckleballer, performed wonderfully out of the bullpen to seal Cardinals wins.

With the Phillies in a tailspin one problem remained—the Cincinnati Reds, who were in first place as the wire approached. The Pirates came to the rescue by shutting out the Reds twice to set up a final wild weekend in which the Cardinals led the Reds by a half game and the Phillies by two and a half. The schedule favored the Redbirds, as they were to play the hapless Mets—who would finish 40 games out of first—while the Reds faced the fading Phillies. Amazingly, the great Bob Gibson was unable to beat Al Jackson of the Mets in the opener, while the Phillies defeated the Reds. The following day the Mets arose again and bit the Cardinals 15–5, while the Reds and Phils were idle. When the Giants lost to the Cubs it became a three-team race going into the final day of the season. The Cardinals (92–69) were even with the Reds and one up on the Phillies (91–70).

The Cardinals pulled ahead of the Mets 5–3 in the fifth as the word came through that Philadelphia had beaten the Reds, 10–0. The Cardinals would either win the pennant or be involved in a three-team tie after 162 games. With Gibson coming out of the bullpen, the Cardinals blew the game open in the late innings and won the organization's ninth pennant and the first in 18 years.

The Cardinals drew the Yankees in the Series. The team had to hold back Gibson until Game 2, having pitched

TRIVIA

Who was the 1964 MVP?

Answers to the trivia questions are on pages 161–162.

him four times in the previous 11 days. The Yankees, behind Whitey Ford, were unable to take advantage, falling to team-leading 20-game winner Ray Sadecki in St. Louis, 9–5. A tired Gibson could not beat Mel Stottlemyre in the second game, and the Yanks squared the Series with an 8–3 win. When Yankee Jim Bouton beat reliever Barney Schultz on a gargantuan Mickey Mantle homer, 2–1, in Game 3, matters looked grim. Then Roger Craig, in relief of Sadecki, evened the Series with a 4–3 win in New York on a Ken Boyer grand slam.

It took 10 innings for Bob Gibson to win Game 5 on a three-run shot from catcher Tim McCarver. After Jim Bouton won Game 6, it was all or nothing for Gibson and Stottlemyre in St. Louis on October 15. On two days' rest, Gibson went the distance for a 7–5 win, and the Cardinals had their seventh World Series triumph.

DID YOU KNOW . . . That Bing Devine went on to become president of the New York Mets during the 1967 season, only to return to St. Louis as GM the following year?

Strangers to the Game

There was no more feared nor more dominant pitcher in baseball during the sixties than Bob Gibson. "Gibson utilized every edge he had as a pitcher," said his longtime battery mate Tim McCarver. "He had a fastball that just exploded in the strike zone." Although a few others—Sandy Koufax, Don Drysdale, and Nolan Ryan, for example—may have thrown harder, according to McCarver, "When Gibson threw the fastball, I could actually feel the heat of the pitch through the glove and the skin and into my bone."

"He was the toughest athlete mentally I ever saw, and the greatest competitor," stated the late, great Cardinals broadcaster Jack Buck, a man who called NFL as well as major league baseball games. The 6'1", 195-pound right-hander's competitive intensity simply knew no bounds. If he felt a hitter was digging in on him, Gibson sent him an inside rocket to remember. He went inside on anyone and everyone. "We played in a time when black people were supposed to stick together," remarked Dick Allen, "so I asked Gibson one time why he always threw at the brothers. He said, 'Because they're the ones who are gonna beat me if I don't.'"

Gibson made himself tough. He was born Pack Robert Gibson on November 9, 1935, in Omaha, Kansas, in extreme poverty, and he was a sickly youth suffering from asthma, rickets, pneumonia, and even a heart murmur. His poor health was likely due in large part to the dual restrictions of racism and poverty in thirties America. Gibson nearly died at age three from either asthma or pneumonia. Nonetheless, he was active in sports and won a basketball scholarship to Creighton University. In 1957 Gibson received a $4,000 bonus to sign with the Cardinals, but he delayed his entry into the Redbirds organization a year to play with the

Bob Gibson struck out 3,117 batters in 17 major league seasons, all with the Cardinals. He won 20 games five times and 251 in his career.

TRIVIA

Who led the Cardinals in hits during the sixties?

Answers to the trivia questions are on pages 161–162.

Harlem Globetrotters. He was a rather slow developer as a professional, not really arriving as a solid star until he was 28 years old.

Gibson's mean persona was intentional. "I wouldn't even say hello to hitters on the other teams, because I didn't want one of them to get the idea that I liked him or something," Gibson explained, "or that, since I'd given him the time of day once, I might not buzz one under his chin." For Gibson, however, it was not about meanness, hate, or any other personally venomous emotion. "My thing was winning," he noted. "I didn't see how being pleasant or amiable had anything to do with winning, so I wasn't pleasant on the mound and I wasn't amiable off it."

Pitching inside—a nearly lost art by the nineties—was also about winning to the cerebral Gibson. "I never hit hitters for the sake of hitting them," he remarked. "That would have had nothing to do with winning, either." Pitching inside was a way of controlling the hitter's intent to take advantage by edging closer to the plate. It sent them a message that they risked getting hit if they moved too close. "Then, while they're mindful of the inside pitch, you throw outside to get the job done."

Gibson was also one of the more outspoken black players of his day. Race was an issue about which he was ready to talk. As such, he was very proud of the unity the 1964 Cardinals displayed. "The men of that team," wrote Curt Flood, "were about as close to being free from that racist poison as a diverse group of 20th-century Americans could possibly be."

The roots of racial harmony were sewn when, with the support of owner August Busch and white stars like Stan Musial and Ken Boyer, the Cardinals desegregated their spring training hotel in St. Petersburg, Florida. In fact, the biracial nature of the hotel during those spring days became a cultural curiosity to locals. "The Cardinals were the rare team that not only believed in each other," stated Gibson, "but genuinely liked each other." The team associated across racial lines away from the ballpark.

Gibson was clearly one of the self-appointed guardians of racial respect. If word of a racial indiscretion arose he or Bill White "would confront the offender directly and make it clear that there would be none of that on the St. Louis Cardinals."

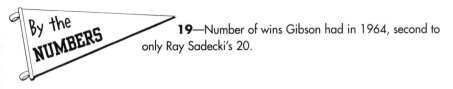

19—Number of wins Gibson had in 1964, second to only Ray Sadecki's 20.

The title of Gibson's autobiography is *Stranger to the Game*, because the Cardinals great has had difficulty getting back into the game, even as a coach. Perhaps it is because he has a bit of a chip on his shoulder, perhaps because he has been too candid, perhaps because he often lacks political correctness. Whatever, as Reggie Smith once said, "The man was going to war when he pitched."

Gibson's teammate Curt Flood was a Cardinals standout in center field, a three-time All-Star and winner of seven consecutive Gold Gloves. In addition, the 5'9", 165-pound Texan compiled a lifetime average of .293 and led the league in hits in the Cardinals' 1964 championship season. Such accomplishments, of course, are not the basis of Curt Flood's fame. After the 1969 season, after a dozen outstanding seasons in St. Louis, the Cardinals traded the 31-year-old to the Philadelphia Phillies.

It seemed, at the time, just another baseball transaction involving a star player heading into the downside of his career. It wasn't. Curt Flood refused to report to Philadelphia, arguing that the reserve clause (which then bound a player to the team holding his contract for his baseball life) prevented him from practicing his profession freely. The dispute made its way to the Supreme Court. Flood lost.

Flood was out of baseball in 1970 but reported to the then–Washington Senators in 1971. He lasted only 13 games.

Although Flood lost his suit in 1972, by 1975 arbitrator Peter Seitz decided that the reserve clause was not binding, paving the way to the free agency flood of money ever since.

For Flood, however, the victory was bittersweet. The players had won, but he had lost his playing career and his welcome in the game. He was a borderline Hall of Fame player but became a pariah. Flood's action seemingly came out of nowhere, surprising many inside and outside the game. Flood later shed light on his motivations, putting it in the context of the times—the turbulent sixties. "Guess you have to understand who that person, who that Curt Flood is," he explained. "I'm a child of the sixties. I'm a man of the sixties. During that period of time this country was coming apart at the seams. We were in Southeast Asia

TRIVIA

Bob Gibson led the
Cardinals in the sixties in
wins with 164. Five pitchers
had between 68 and 61
wins in the decade. Can
you name them?

Answers to the trivia questions are on pages 161–162.

[involved in the Vietnam conflict]. Good men were dying for America and the Constitution. In the southern part of the United States we were marching for civil rights, and Dr. King had been assassinated, and we lost the Kennedys. And to think that merely because I was a professional baseball player, I could ignore what was going on outside the walls of Busch Stadium was truly hypocrisy, and now I found that all of those rights that these great Americans were dying for, I didn't have in my own profession."

Flood stood alone in 1975. Today, however, every major league player owes his good fortune in large part to none other than Curt Flood, who challenged the reigning baseball power structure. Yet, the game—the players association, the Hall of Fame, the writers—has offered Flood no official recognition for his role in effecting this revolution in baseball. Only 59 years old, he died in 1997, still a stranger to the game.

And More

The 1964 Cardinals appeared to be one-year wonders as the team plummeted to a desultory 80–81 record the following season, despite a 20–12 campaign by Gibson. On May 12, 1966, the Cardinals left old Busch Stadium (formerly Sportsman's Park) behind and opened new Busch Stadium with a 4–3, 12-inning conquest of Atlanta. That and hosting the All-Star Game were among the few highlights of an 83–79 year, good enough for sixth in the 10-team NL. This despite another strong 21–12 year by Gibson.

It was the second ho-hum season under new skipper Red Schoendienst, who had succeeded the popular Johnny Keane. He was let go by the Yanks before he had completed even two years at the New York throttle, before coming to St. Louis.

In 1967 Bob Gibson broke his leg and won only 13 games. That was the bad news. The good news was that Dick Hughes—in his first full year in the majors—went 16–6, another first-full-year man named Steve Carlton was 14–9, and third-year man Nelson Briles rebounded from a 4–15 year and turned in a 14–5 campaign. Toss in a 10–7 year from veteran Ray Washburn, and the St. Louis Cardinals had 67 of what turned out to be 101 wins in another pennant-winning campaign.

The big story, however, was not on the mound. It was at first base. With Bill White gone to Philadelphia, the Redbirds had acquired Orlando Cepeda from the Giants. Cepeda, anxious to recover his reputation as a superstar after an injury-plagued final season in the Bay, hit .303 in 123 games after joining St. Louis in May 1966. In 1967 the 29-year-old Cepeda batted .325, hammered 25 home runs, and knocked in 111 runs in a pitching-dominated era to become the unanimous pick for MVP.

The 1967 Series was no less exciting than the one three years previous. This time the Cardinals faced the Red Sox and Triple Crown MVP Carl Yastrzemski. It looked like a mismatch as the Cardinals jumped off to a three-games-to-one lead. The Red Sox took Game 5, 3–1, behind Cy Young ace Jim Lonborg, and when they prevailed at Fenway, 8–4, in Game 6, it was down to the nub once again.

Gibson and Lonborg, each with two wins, would face each other for all of the 1967 marbles. It looked even except for one thing: Gibson was pitching on (what was then normal) three days' rest, Lonborg on just two. It showed, and the Cardinals rolled to an easy 7–2 victory behind Gibson.

The Cardinals of 1968 were no longer the also-ran Cardinals, but rather a team that had claimed two World Series in four years and was

The 1968 season was Bob Gibson's crescendo. He powered his way to a league-leading 268 strikeouts, 13 shutouts, and a postage-stamp-sized ERA of 1.12. In Game 1 of the 1968 World Series, he set a postseason record with 17 strikeouts; included in that total is Detroit's Willie Horton (above).

DID YOU KNOW ...
That Hall of Famer Red Schoendienst played his entire career with a visual defect? A staple flew into his left eye when he was a teenager. It was serious enough that a physician suggested the eye be removed, but Schoendienst, wanting to play baseball, refused. With the eye never corrected, he adjusted his stance as a switch-hitter such that his head was turned toward the pitcher in a way that even when batting right-handed he could see the pitch leave the pitcher's hand with his right eye.

loaded with talent in the persons of Cepeda, Brock, McCarver, Curt Flood, Mike Shannon, and Gibson to name several. St. Louis had swagger, and in 1968 another pennant, as they romped to a 97–65 record, fully nine games better than the distant San Francisco Giants.

The 1968 season was the year of the pitcher, as the National League ERA was a microscopic 2.99. Bob Gibson, however, made that number seem inflationary as he turned in a 1.12 mark to back a 22–9 season. It was the best mark since the dead-ball era. He fired 13 shutouts and allowed just 38 earned runs in 305 innings. His year was so dominant he won both the Cy Young and the MVP awards. Gibson was backed by Briles, Carlton, and Washburn, who together added 46 wins.

It was all pitching, as the Redbirds scored just 583 runs all season—112 fewer than in 1967—an average of just 3.6 per contest. No Cardinal hit more than 16 home runs and no Redbird managed an excess of 79 RBIs. Curt Flood's .301 average won the team batting title by 22 points.

The Cardinals were prohibitive favorites against the AL champions from Detroit. Moreover, the big story was the pitching collision between Gibson and Denny McLain, who won an incredible 31 games against just six losses, wrapped around a meager 1.96 ERA. (Amazingly, McLain's ERA ranked fourth in the AL, which had a 2.98 average.) St. Louis made short work of the Tigers early, going up three games to one with Gibson besting McLain in both the first and the fourth games. The Tigers claimed the fifth game behind lefty Mickey Lolich, who won his second game, this

TRIVIA

Ken Boyer led the Cardinals in home runs with 141 and RBIs with 595 during the decade. Who was second in each category?

Answers to the trivia questions are on pages 161–162.

All-Sixties Cardinals Team

Position	Player
First Base	Bill White
Second Base	Julian Javier
Third Base	Ken Boyer
Shortstop	Dick Groat
Left Field	Lou Brock
Center Field	Curt Flood
Right Field	Mike Shannon
Pitcher	Bob Gibson
Catcher	Tim McCarver
Manager	Red Schoendienst

time 5–3. With McLain rocked in Game 4 and leaving in the third, Tigers skipper Mayo Smith brought the maverick right-hander back in the sixth game, which he won in a 13–1 blowout in St. Louis.

It was game number seven again. This time Gibson took on Lolich, the latter on two days' rest. Despite recording 8 strikeouts to set a Series record of 35, Gibson could not shake the left-handed Lolich, who picked Flood and Brock off first in the sixth. In the seventh, Jim Northrup delivered a three-bagger to send home two Tigers mates, and 1968 belonged to Detroit.

The 1969 season brought divisional play. With Roger Maris, who had been a stellar member of the 1967 and 1968 champions, retired and Cepeda off to Atlanta, the shaken Cardinals did not rebound from their Series disappointment, finishing 87–75 and in fourth place in the six-team NL East. Gibson, with a 20–13 record, was a key factor in the team's staying above .500.

Kings of the Ozarks

Many things make a franchise famous, not the least of which are public relations and publicity, and no one did more to put the St. Louis Cardinals on baseball fans' maps than Harry Christopher Carabina, better known as Harry Caray. From 1945 to 1969 Harry Caray was the voice of the Cardinals. His was a radio play-by-play era, one in which announcers had to paint a "word's-eye view" of the action, and none did it with greater excitement than Harry Caray. Announcing on St. Louis' powerful KMOX, Caray's broadcasts could be heard throughout the Midwest by fans who loved the excitement he created.

Born March 1, 1914, in St. Louis, Caray was a semipro baseball player before getting into radio. He learned his craft at stations in Joliet, Illinois, and Kalamazoo, Michigan, and was once a colleague of a young newscaster named Paul Harvey. Caray did St. Louis Hawks NBA games as well as University of Missouri football, but baseball was his passion and the Cardinals were his team.

Caray was orphaned in his youth, possessed an addictive personality, and developed an insatiable thirst for approval and attention. Blessed with boundless energy, he found the microphone to be both his best friend and his avenue to fame. Caray was not at all from the Red Barber school of broadcasting. Barber, longtime and beloved voice of the Brooklyn Dodgers, believed the announcer's job was to report the game as objectively as possible, avoiding unnecessary displays of emotion. The estimable Vin Scully, who learned at Barber's knee, is one of the best examples of broadcast "Barberism." Harry Caray was the polar opposite. A shameless homer, but never above criticizing the locals if their play was deficient, Caray announced from the passionate fan's point of view.

That Pete Gray—not a Cardinals player—was perhaps the most famous player in St. Louis during the 1945 season? The Browns outfielder lost his right arm in a childhood accident and learned to play with great dexterity despite the limitation. The 28-year-old Gray appeared in 77 games and hit .218 in 234 at-bats. Born Peter Wyshner, Gray disappeared from the major leagues after that one war year.

"It's the fans that need spring training," Caray once remarked. "You gotta get 'em interested. Wake 'em up and let 'em know that their season is coming, the good times are gonna roll." And wake them up he did, never forgetting that it was the fans who purchased the tickets, bought the beer, and tuned in to the radio. "I know it is the fans that are responsible for me being here," he said. "I've always tried in each and every broadcast to serve the fans to the best of my ability."

Caray was the voice of the Cardinals for a quarter of a century. He would occasionally get into spats with players because of his open displeasure with substandard play. The fans, however, loved him because they trusted the integrity of his calls, his unwillingness to color things red for the Cardinals when the team's play did not warrant such a tilt. This and his infectiously friendly, extremely enthusiastic style made Caray as much a star as the players on whom he reported, a fame he cherished and nurtured at every opportunity.

Caray defended his pro-fans approach, saying, "If a fan had a chance to get behind a mike like I do, he would sound like I do."

His two trademark calls were "Holy cow!" when something exciting occurred and "It might be. It could be. It is—a home run. Holy cow!"

In 1969 Caray left St. Louis over a personal rift with the Busch family, one kept very quiet by all parties. He spent a year in Oakland, announcing for Charlie Finley's A's, and then it was on to Chicago—11 years with the White Sox and 16 with the Cubs, where Caray became even more famous. Caray had a listed phone number and a readiness to sign any autograph or pose for any picture at a fan's request.

He suffered a stroke in the late eighties, and although slowed and prevented from drinking his beloved Budweiser, he came back and did the Cubs games until his death just before the 1998 season.

When Caray left St. Louis, the team had a more-than-adequate replacement in Jack Buck, who shared the Cardinals booth with Caray in

1954. Though less extroverted than Caray, John Francis Buck, born in Holyoke, Massachusetts, was the quintessential professional announcer, one with a pleasing voice and an excellent command of the English language. He knew when to inject enthusiasm and when to hold back—always on pace. Buck, who died in 2002, received the Hall of Fame's Ford Frick Award in 1987, while the more famous Caray was honored in 1989.

Both have heirs who have pressed on. Caray's son, the more droll Skip Caray, has long been the voice of the Atlanta Braves, while Skip's son, Chip, who is more like Harry in style, picked up the fallen mike from his grandfather in Chicago in 1998 and has since moved on to Atlanta.

From 1945 to 1969 Harry Caray, shown here interviewing manager Harry Walker in 1955, was the voice of the St. Louis Cardinals. He called games that could be heard all over the Midwest on powerful KMOX with a style that was both shameless in its advocacy of the home team and honest in its assessment of the how the team was playing.

As for Buck, his son Joe became the voice of the Cardinals as well as national baseball telecasts, often paired with Tim McCarver.

Harry Caray—outspoken, opinionated, outrageous, exciting—and Jack Buck—professional, thorough, first-rate—are cornerstone figures in building Cardinals fandom. Buck cherished the memories of working with Caray. "When Harry and I were doing the games together, we were as good a team as there ever was," noted the usually modest Buck. "His style and mine were so different that it made for a balanced broadcast. The way we approached the job, with the interest and love both of us had for the game, made our work kind of special."

Indeed it was. Cardinals fans nationwide become nostalgic when they recall hearing, on hot summer nights, the husky voice of Caray giving his greeting: "Hello, everybody, this is Harry Caray and Jack Buck . . ."

TRIVIA

Sam Breadon was the Cardinals president from 1920 to 1947. Only one man served as the team's president for longer. Who was he?

Answers to the trivia questions are on pages 161–162.

Lifetime Achievements

The times were a changin' in 1970, nationally, as well as with the St. Louis Cardinals. The unsettling sixties—to which Curt Flood referred—were gone. It was a decade that saw the assassination of President John and Senator Robert Kennedy in addition to Martin Luther King Jr. A war in Southeast Asia that started with wide popular support had melted the country down to such a state that a once powerful President Lyndon Johnson all but abdicated his presidency. Violence had filled the city streets in every major city, including St. Louis, as African Americans became vocal and hostile over the lack of equal opportunity across the nation. A dissident faction of American youth made their presence known in disruptive protests on college campuses nationwide.

The impact of the sixties was felt in major league baseball as well, as black athletes such as Flood, Gibson, and White became powerful spokespeople on issues of inequity in baseball. It was not a comfortable time, not an era of good feeling, despite the comparatively harmonious spirit on the Cardinals teams of the decade. Nonetheless, for Cardinals fans the sixties brought some escape from the cruel realities of war and national civil disorder. Their beloved Cardinals snared three pennants and two World Series, and despite occasionally uncomfortable boat-rocking political statements by players, the Cardinals seemed to experience less discontent than many other less successful franchises.

By 1970 the nation seemed weary of confrontation, and with Nixon in the White House, a less tumultuous, more tightly controlled environment seemed to be taking hold, at least outside baseball. As for the Redbirds, Harry Caray was gone and so were the championship seasons and a number of the players from those great teams, including Ken Boyer, Bill White, and Orlando Cepeda to name a few. More important,

On August 29, 1977, Cardinals legend Lou Brock (No. 20), who came to the Redbirds in a lopsided trade with the Cubs during the stretch drive in 1964, broke Ty Cobb's career stolen-base record by swiping number 893 against the Padres.

however, Curt Flood, the Cardinals mainstay in center field, was gone but surely not quietly. He had been dealt to Philadelphia, a city to which he did not want to go in part because of his feelings about the racial climate there. Flood refused to report to the Phillies and appealed to Commissioner Bowie Kuhn, claiming that the binding nature of the reserve clause (the rule that sealed a player for life to the team holding his contract, giving the player essentially zero bargaining power as he played through a series of one-year contracts) turned players into slaves, albeit well-paid ones. This was typical sixties explosive language, particularly coming from an African-American player, and as such disturbed many traditionalists in the game. Nevertheless, Flood's position created an unsettled air in baseball in general, and in St. Louis in particular.

Kuhn rejected Flood's claim, and the case made its way through the courts until the Supreme Court upheld the reserve clause, a condition that would last only five years.

TRIVIA

Keith Hernandez shared the 1979 MVP with which player?

Answers to the trivia questions are on pages 161–162.

By the midseventies the game was turned upside down, as free agency kicked in and no longer did a player long to be a $100,000 ballplayer—six-figure multiyear pacts became common.

The Cardinals had more to worry about than the Flood grievance, as the team tumbled to a 76–86 fourth-place finish in the NL East, a six-team division created in 1969 consisting of the Cubs, Mets, Pirates, Phillies, and Montreal Expos (an expansion franchise birthed the previous season). No one was happy, including Bullet Bob Gibson, who won his second Cy Young Award with a 23–7 mark. Troubled slugger Dick Allen, a highly charismatic, on-the-edge black athlete whom the Cardinals had received in exchange for Flood, complained about the artificial turf in the new Busch Stadium, claiming, "If a horse can't eat it, I don't want to play on it." Despite Allen's All-Star season that included 34 homers and 101 RBIs, manager Schoendienst, perhaps longing for more peaceful times, wasn't crazy about having Allen play for him on any surface, especially given Allen's already stormy past, all of which filled the clubhouse with tension.

All-Seventies Cardinals Team

Position	Player
First Base	Keith Hernandez
Second Base	Mike Tyson
Third Base	Joe Torre
Shortstop	Garry Templeton
Left Field	Lou Brock
Center Field	Bake McBride
Right Field	George Hendrick
Pitcher	Bob Gibson
Catcher	Ted Simmons
Manager	Red Schoendienst

That Lou Brock hit 149 home runs in his 19-year career: 102 in the sixties and only 47 in the seventies?

Allen's sojourn in St. Louis lasted one season before he was peddled to Los Angeles. With a more peaceful clubhouse and slugging third baseman Joe Torre hitting a whopping .363 en route to the NL MVP, the Cards rebounded in 1971 to a 90–72 finish behind the world champion Pittsburgh Pirates. On the mound, young Steve Carlton began supplanting the aging Gibson, winning 20 games for the Redbirds. The southpaw had a vicious slider to go with a steaming fastball, which struck out a then-record 19 Mets in a game on September 15, 1969.

The optimism of 1971 evaporated in a dismal 75–81 season the following year, one in which the traded Carlton won 27 games for a Philadelphia club that would win but 59 of 156 games in a season delayed by an owner-player labor dispute. By 1973 the big stories involved the lifetime achievements of aging players like Brock and Gibson. Brock picked up his 600th stolen base, 2,000[th] hit, and 1,000[th] RBI, as the Cardinals divided 162 games evenly. Because of the incredible mediocrity of the NL East, however, that 81–81 mark left St. Louis an agonizing game and a half behind the "champion" Mets at 82–79.

In 1974 the Cardinals improved to 86–75, but the Pirates went 88–74 to make it a second consecutive game-and-a-half shortfall in the East. More achievements included Brock breaking Maury Wills' single-season stolen-base record with 118, Bake McBride earning the Rookie of the Year award, and Gibson fanning his 3,000[th] hitter, putting him behind only Walter Johnson as the all-time K king. The next year would be Gibson's last, leaving him 251 wins and a day in his honor at Busch during an 82–80 season. He had led the Cardinals in wins in the seventies with 84, followed by Bob Forsch with 72. The 1976 season would be Schoendienst's last as well, as the team skidded to a 72–90 finish, but Red finished having won two pennants, in 1967 and 1968.

TRIVIA

Who led the Cardinals in home runs in the seventies?

Answers to the trivia questions are on pages 161–162.

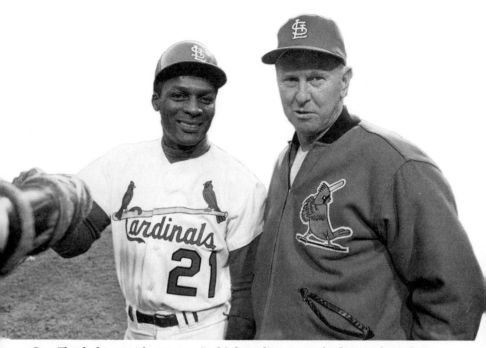

Curt Flood, shown with manager Red Schoendienst, was the first modern player to challenge baseball's reserve clause, which bound each player to his current team until he was either traded or released. When Flood was traded to the Phillies during the off-season in 1969, he refused to report, citing his objections to playing in Philadelphia.

Vern Rapp steered the Cards to a better 83–79 mark in 1977 but was gone in favor of first Jack Krol, then Ken Boyer before the close of a disastrous 69–93 1978 season. Brock pushed on, however, breaking Ty Cobb's career stolen-base record with number 893 in late 1977. The decade closed with Brock—in his final season—registering his 3,000th hit in a game against the Cubs and swiping a then all-time record 938 bases, as the Cardinals with new manager Ken Boyer and new stars like catcher Ted Simmons and first baseman Keith Hernandez gave fans hope with an 86–76 finish.

A Trip across I-70

Whitey Herzog appeared to have it made in Kansas City. He took over the managerial reins of the Royals late in the 1975 season and steered them to 41 wins in 66 games. He then topped that by winning the AL West divisional title the next three seasons, averaging just short of 95 wins per season. But the candid, colorful, outspoken Herzog was very unpopular in the Ewing Kauffman family. That was not a good thing, because Kauffman owned the Kansas City Royals. Hence, when the Royals went 85–77 in 1979, finishing second in the West, Herzog found himself unemployed going into the 1980 season.

Meanwhile, if you were to get on Interstate 70 and drive across the state to St. Louis, it would become quickly apparent that the wheels were coming off the Cardinals wagon. After a promising (86–76) 1979 season under Ken Boyer, the team—with its starting staff beset by injuries—stumbled out of the gate going 18–33 and costing the beloved Boyer his perch in the Cardinals roost. Jack Krol managed the team for one losing game, half as long as his two-day reign in 1978 when he went 1–1. With the team at 18–34, owner Gussie Busch had had enough and turned to none other than Whitey Herzog.

The 48-year-old Dorrel Norman Elvert Herzog quickly took a trip across I-70 and restored order, going an optimistic 38–35 from early June to late August before temporarily handing the reins over to Red Schoendienst for the rest of the season. Despite his rather immediate success, Herzog did not like the 1980 team one bit. "I've never seen such a bunch of misfits," he noted in his insightful and entertaining autobiography, *White Rat.* "Nobody would run out a ball. Nobody in the bullpen wanted the ball. We had guys on drugs—and another guy who sneaked off into the tunnel between innings so he could take a hit of vodka."

Whitey Herzog (right) won 822 games as manager of the Cards, including three first-place finishes and one championship.

For Herzog all this was inexcusable, despite his awareness that the drug culture of the sixties and seventies had infected a number of baseball franchises. "I don't have a whole lot of rules as a manager," he explained, "but one thing I insist on is that players run as hard a they can all of the time. That was going to be a new experience for some of the Cardinals players."

When Busch asked Herzog, who had also been made the general manager, for an assessment of the club, Whitey let him have it. He told the owner he had a bunch of prima donnas, overpaid bums on the payroll, guys who would never win a thing. "You've got a bunch of mean people, some sorry human beings," he went on. "It's the first time I've ever been scared to walk through my own clubhouse. We've got drug problems, we've got ego problems, and we ain't ever going anywhere."

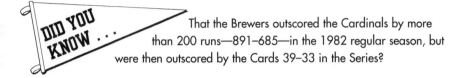

That the Brewers outscored the Cardinals by more than 200 runs—891–685—in the 1982 regular season, but were then outscored by the Cards 39–33 in the Series?

Having gotten the green light from Busch, Herzog set about remaking the Cardinals, who played in a then-cavernous Busch Stadium, into a team built on speed, defense, and pitching. He opened the 1981 season with a whole new look. Darrell Porter, who had been Herzog's catcher in Kansas City, was catching. Tommy Herr was at second, with Ken Oberkfell moved to third. Most important, however, Herzog acquired Bruce Sutter, the game's preeminent closer, from the Cubs as his "door-slammer."

The 1981 season was bizarre. The Cardinals posted the best record in the NL East but did not make the playoffs because of a strike that wiped out the middle third of the season. Commissioner Kuhn, in an attempt at a creative resolution, decided to split the season in halves, with the team having the best first-half record playing the team with the best second-half mark in a preliminary playoff round. Because the Phillies led at the strike point and the Expos had the best post-strike mark, the 59–43 Cardinals were out, and Herzog was not happy.

Nevertheless, there was work to do on the transaction front, and Herzog did it. Among other things, he moved quickly to pick up a young glove from the Padres named Ozzie Smith, trading away Garry Templeton, and then pulled in Lonnie Smith from the Phillies by way of Cleveland.

Now that Herzog had his team—one with blazing speed, excellent defense, and tough pitching—he stepped down as general manager, leaving that job to Joe McDonald. He also had the Cardinals' 13th pennant, as the team scooted to a 92–70 mark in 1982 to claim the NL East. After sweeping Atlanta in the playoffs, the Cardinals faced the Robin Yount and Paul Molitor–led Milwaukee Brewers in the World Series. The fall classic would match Milwaukee's run-scoring machine with Herzog's club that led the NL in stolen bases (200) and

TRIVIA

Which big-name relief pitcher did Herzog acquire and then trade once he had Sutter?

Answers to the trivia questions are on pages 161–162.

fewest runs allowed (609) and had posted a third-ranked 3.37 ERA. After being clubbed to death, 10–0, in the opener by Harvey's Wallbangers, the nickname given to Harvey Kuenn's offensive powerhouse, the Cardinals survived Game 2, 5–4, to square the classic. Entering Game 6 in St. Louis, however, the Brewers held a 3–2 Series lead.

Game 6 was all Cardinals, 13–1, and so, once again, the Redbirds were in a for-all-the-marbles seventh game. Trailing 3–1 in the bottom of the sixth, the Cardinals rallied for three runs, then added another pair in the eighth, as they cruised to a 6–3 victory and the organization's ninth World Series title. Darrell Porter was named both NL playoff and Series MVP.

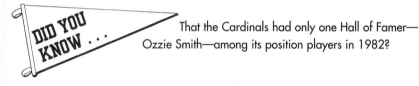

DID YOU KNOW . . . That the Cardinals had only one Hall of Famer—Ozzie Smith—among its position players in 1982?

Whitey Ball

A competitive and exciting Cardinals team proved too inconsistent to win in 1983, as the team finished a disappointing fourth in the NL East. It wasn't as bad as it looked; the Redbirds were but a half a game out on September 5 but then struggled on a 13-game road trip, finishing the campaign 79–83. Cardinals mound mainstays Joaquin Andujar and Bob Forsch, who had combined for 30 wins in 1982, were only able to garner 16 together in 1983. There were other problems. Herzog suspected that star first baseman Keith Hernandez, who in the manager's opinion was not hustling, was involved in drugs and had him moved to the Mets.

The 1984 season was a bit of a reverse. After an agonizingly slow start, the team rallied after the All-Star break, but it was too late to catch the Cubs, who would win the East and appear in their first postseason series since 1945. St. Louis ended the season with an 84–78 record. As if two so-so years were not enough, the team lost Bruce Sutter to Atlanta and free agency after the season.

Just when things looked darkest, Whitey Ball kicked in. The 1985 Cardinals hit only 87 homers but ran out 59 triples, drew 586 walks, and swiped 314 bases to lead the league in runs scored (747) and capture the NL East title with a 101–61 log. Willie McGee blossomed into a star, leading the league in hitting at .353, while the young speedster Vince Coleman stole 110 bases. Second sacker Tommy Herr had only 49 extra-base hits—8 of which were home runs—and yet clutch hit his way to 110 RBIs, and new first baseman Jack Clark slugged 22 homers in 126 games. On the mound Andujar and John Tudor each won 21 and Danny Cox 18 more, for a team that finished second in the NL with an ERA of 3.10.

Despite all this, the real Cardinals baseball excitement of 1985 was still ahead. First up were Tommy Lasorda's Los Angeles Dodgers, winners

TOP TEN — Whitey Quotes

Bill James once said something to the effect that Herzog *fortunately* lacked the good sense to keep his opinions to himself. It is fortunate indeed, as the following Whiteyisms indicate.

1. "Baseball has been good to me since I quit trying to play it."
2. "If you don't have outstanding relief pitching, you might as well [urinate] on the fire and call the dogs."
3. "I'm not buddy-buddy with the players. If they need a buddy, let them buy a dog."
4. "Some people asked me if I would be interested in managing the A's. I said a definite no, thank you. At night, that place is a graveyard with lights."
5. "The way we have been playing, I might tell my players not to cross the picket line [during the 1979 umpires strike]."
6. "We need three kinds of pitching: left-handed, right-handed, and relief."
7. "The only way to make money as a manager is to win in one place, get fired and hired somewhere else."
8. "A sense of humor and a good bullpen [are the keys to being a good manager]."
9. When octogenarian owner Gussie Busch spoke of granting the successful Herzog a lifetime contract with the Cardinals, Herzog had one question: "Your lifetime or mine?"
10. "I think my plan [to reduce the roster size to 22 and add two expansion teams] is sensible and practical, which probably means it's doomed."

of the West for the sixth time in the previous 12 years. L.A. broke out to a 2–0 NLCS lead, beating Tudor and Andujar in the first two games and leaving the Cardinals' hopes in tatters. Herzog decided to go with 25-year-old Danny Cox in Game 3. Cox, who had posted a glittering 2.88 ERA to back his 18 wins, held the Dodgers to a pair of runs through six innings. The Cardinals, however, had gathered four of their own in the first two frames, and that was enough for a 4–2 triumph. Tudor came back in Game 4 and coasted to a 12–2 Redbirds win.

Game 5 in St. Louis was a grinder. With the score locked at two apiece in the bottom of the ninth, switch-hitting Ozzie Smith lifted his first-ever round-tripper from the left side to put the Cardinals on top 3–2. Back in L.A., the Dodgers rallied in Game 6, registering a 4–1 lead after six. After the Cardinals got three of their own in the seventh to tie the tilt at four, Los Angeles' Mike Marshall slugged an eighth-inning homer to give the Dodgers a 5–4 edge. In the ninth, however, Jack Clark delivered a three-run circuit shot to hand the Cardinals the game and their 14th pennant.

No one played shortstop with more competency—and flair—than first-ballot Hall of Famer Ozzie Smith, who earned 13 Gold Gloves in his 19 seasons with the Cardinals.

DID YOU KNOW . . . That the Cardinals led the league in stolen bases seven straight times beginning in 1982?

The fall classic figured to be special. It matched Herzog with his old team, the Kansas City Royals, then managed by Dick Howser, in what was called the I-70 Series.

The Cardinals made it look easy as they swept the first two games in Kansas City by 3–1 and 4–2 scores. They all but broke the Royals' spirit in Game 2 by rallying for four runs in the ninth to turn an impending 2–0 loss into a win. Bret Saberhagen flattened the Redbirds in the third game, 6–1, but St. Louis rebounded for a 3–0 triumph behind Tudor in the next one. It was then all St. Louis at three games to one. Facing elimination, the Royals backed Danny Jackson with six runs to pull within a game of the Cardinals, winning Game 5 6–1.

The Series moved to Kansas City. Danny Cox was brilliant, shutting the Royals out through seven, while receiving but a single run from his teammates. When Ken Dayley finished the eighth for the Redbirds, the score was still 1–0 St. Louis.

In the ninth, Herzog turned the game over to young Todd Worrell, a flame-throwing right-hander who had begun the season as a starter for the Cardinals' Louisville farm team, managed by Jim Fregosi. Worrell had been outstanding after coming up in late August and seemed destined for greatness as a closer.

Worrell induced pinch-hitter Jorge Orta to hit a bounder to Jack Clark at first. Clark flipped the ball to Worrell covering first for the out. But wait! First-base umpire Don Denkinger ruled Orta safe, and the Royals had the tying run aboard. "The throw beat Orta by half a step," wrote Herzog in his autobiography, "a close play but the kind of play the umpire calls right 999 out of 1,000 times. This was the thousandth time." Clearly Denkinger had missed the call, something he admitted later, but there was no erasing the runner or registering the out.

Nonetheless, the Cardinals had not lost a game in the ninth all season long,

TRIVIA

What was the Cardinals bullpen called after Sutter left in 1985?

Answers to the trivia questions are on pages 161–162.

By the NUMBERS

3—Number of major awards Cardinals players copped for 1985—two for regular-season play and one for the postseason. Willie McGee was the NL MVP, Vince Coleman was the NL Rookie of the Year, and Ozzie Smith was the NLCS MVP.

and they didn't figure to lose this one when the Royals' Steve Balboni hit a foul pop to first. More bad news: Clark failed to make the play. Balboni got a single. A passed ball and an intentional walk followed, and with the bases loaded, former Cardinal Dane Iorg, one of Whitey's favorites who hit .541 for the Redbirds in the 1982 Series, stepped in to pinch hit. Iorg hit a flare to right that fell safely, and the Royals scored a pair to tie the Series at three games apiece.

The Cardinals were down, and despite having another game to atone for the loss, they were out. "The players had their heads on their chest," said Herzog. "There was no fire in their eyes. I called a meeting before the game, tried to give them a pep talk. I hardly ever do that, and I guess my lack of practice showed. We had nothing."

The Royals came up with 11, and the 11–0 whitewash ended the Cardinals' otherwise brilliant year in the most bitter of ways. But Denkinger suffered worse than anyone. After the game, he was supposed to go out for dinner. He couldn't. He couldn't even read a newspaper or watch television that evening, the call affected him so much. He was not immune to the Cardinals' rage, either. Denkinger received hundreds of pieces of hate mail and even death threats, necessitating round-the-clock police and FBI protection. Nonetheless, in retrospect Herzog felt for him. "Here's Donny Denkinger," wrote Whitey, "a guy I've known for years and a guy I regard as one of the top five or six umpires in the major leagues. A veteran umpire, he misses one call, and suddenly he's famous. He gets a big write-up in *Sports Illustrated* and the newspapers all for making a mistake."

Room for One More

When the Cardinals were swept by the Mets in a four-game set in April 1986, little did they realize their fate was to be doomed in the East by those very New Yorkers, who finished the season with two out of three for the year—108 wins against just 54 losses. In St. Louis, the worst team in the NL that May—the club had won only nine games—the bickering and feuding Cards went down to a 36–50 mark at the All-Star break. The second half, however, was a different story. The Redbirds went 43–32 to close the season three games under .500 at 79–82. Nonetheless, it was a disillusioning season, something reflected in Herzog's diary on October 6. "It's over. It ended in the dark yesterday afternoon in Chicago. Thank God they have never installed lights in Wrigley Field [they did in 1988], or else we would have had to play the second game of a doubleheader on the last day of the season."

The toilet flushed—the Cardinals were back to Whitey Ball in 1987, as the team roared through the NL East with a 95–67 record, three games ahead of the reigning champion Mets, despite being beset by injuries for the second straight year.

The Cardinals sent 11–11 Greg Mathews to the mound in the NLCS opener in St. Louis against the San Francisco Giants, and he bested Giants ace Rick Reuschel in a 5–3 Redbirds win. Clutch pitcher Dave Dravecky shut St. Louis and John Tudor out by a 5–0 verdict in Game 2. With St. Louis winning the next one but losing Game 4 the series moved to a fifth game in San Francisco, one pitting Mathews against Reuschel once again. A four-run fourth-inning uprising powered the Giants to a 6–3 win, with Dravecky ready to go for Game 6 in St. Louis.

Only 11 hits and one run were registered in that game—Dravecky and Tudor being absolutely brilliant—but, fortunately, the Cardinals

All-Eighties Cardinals Team

Position	Player
First Base	Jack Clark
Second Base	Tom Herr
Third Base	Terry Pendleton
Shortstop	Ozzie Smith
Left Field	Vince Coleman
Center Field	Willie McGee
Right Field	George Hendrick
Pitcher	Bob Forsch
Catcher	Darrell Porter
Manager	Whitey Herzog

were on the right side of the numbers and took the win on a second-inning tally that stood up for the final seven frames. When the Redbirds exploded for four runs in the second inning of the deciding game, the pennant belonged in St. Louis for the 15th time as the Cardinals romped to a 6–0 victory behind Danny Cox.

World Series games never seem to be easy for St. Louis, and the 1987 classic was no different. With Minnesota ready to throw their two-man pitching tandem of Frank Viola and Bert Blyleven as many as five times in a seven-game Series, the Cardinals lost the opener 10–1 to Viola in the Metrodome. When Blyleven won an 8–4 verdict in the dome in Game 2, the backs of the Redbirds were scratching the wall. Back in St. Louis, Tudor pitched a 3–1 gem in Game 3, and the Cards got to Viola for a 7–2 win behind Bob Forsch in relief of Mathews in Game 4. Suddenly the food tasted better in Cardinalville. With Cox beating Blyleven 4–2 in the next one, it tasted excellent, especially considering John Tudor was ready for the clincher in Game 6.

Reality sometimes bites, however. With St. Louis up 5–2 in the fifth, the hometowners broke loose for four runs. They followed that with four more in the sixth to win 11–5 and force a deciding Game 7 in Minnesota—one

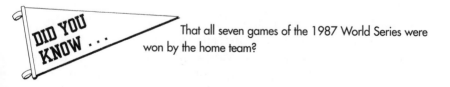

DID YOU KNOW . . . That all seven games of the 1987 World Series were won by the home team?

that would favor Minnesota, with Viola facing fellow southpaw, rookie Joe Magrane. With the Cardinals up 2–1 in the bottom of the fifth, the Twins managed a run to tie the score. They got one more off reliever Danny Cox in the sixth, and that proved enough in a 4–2 Series clincher.

That was the end of the glorious Cardinals run of the eighties. The 1988 squad, once again riddled with injuries, was never in the race, going 76–86. When injuries crippled the Redbirds' starting staff early in 1989, matters looked even grimmer. Nonetheless, the team hung on and was within a half game of the front-running Cubs on the strength of a come-from-behind win on September 8. A six-game losing skid followed, however, and the team settled for third in the East at 86–76.

The new decade brought little happiness for Herzog, who ranks third among Cardinals managers in wins. With the team at 33–47, and going nowhere, Whitey, with one Manager of the Year award to his credit, turned in his managerial keys and resigned, ending as exciting and memorable an era as any in Cardinals lore.

A Rough Start to an Unforgettable Decade

Trusty Cardinals loyalist Red Schoendienst filled in for 24 games, winning 13, while the Cardinals waited to install their next manager. As it turned out, the Ol' Redhead was the only skipper who enjoyed success that year, as Joe Torre began his career at the Redbirds helm by going 24–34 to close 1990.

The next year the team jumped to an 84–78 mark and a second-place finish. The following two campaigns, however, were much the same at 83–79 and then 87–75. Among the highlights of those three seasons were Lee Smith leading the NL in saves in both 1991 and 1992, with 47 and 43, respectively, and Mark Whiten hitting four home runs in a single game on September 7, 1993, against Cincinnati. He was only the 12th player in major league history to accomplish the feat, and his 12 RBIs tied a one-game record held by fellow Cardinal Jim Bottomley.

In 1994 the first half of the decade ended with two major events affecting the Cardinals. First, the team was moved to the Central Division in the newly realigned, three division NL. Second, the team completed play on August 12 with a 53–61 mark, as a work stoppage ended the 1994 season and wiped out the World Series. A 20–27 start brought an end to the Joe Torre era in St. Louis in 1995. Mike Jorgensen took the team the rest of the way with a 42–54 mark.

Off the field there was even bigger news, as the Cardinals ended their longtime alliance with Anheuser-Busch. The team was sold to a group of well-heeled Cardinals fans led by Fred Hanser, William DeWitt Jr., and Andrew Baur.

The Cardinals had a new look in 1996. Busch Stadium was revamped, with natural grass among the changes. Moreover, the team hired Tony La Russa, fresh from Oakland where he won three straight

Tony La Russa joined the Cardinals as manager in 1996 and has been winning nonstop since then. Outfielder Jim Edmonds has averaged more than 35 home runs per year since being traded to the Cardinals in 2000.

All-Nineties
Cardinals Team

Position	Player
First Base	Mark McGwire
Second Base	Jose Oquendo
Third Base	Todd Zeile
Shortstop	Ozzie Smith
Left Field	Ron Gant
Center Field	Ray Lankford
Right Field	Brian Jordan
Pitcher	Bob Tewksbury
Catcher	Tom Pagnozzi
Manager	Tony La Russa

AL pennants and one World Series. The year also brought the return of fan-favorite Willie McGee and the final season of future Hall of Famer Ozzie Smith.

La Russa pulled a major PR bone in his inaugural season by playing Royce Clayton at shortstop ahead of Smith. This both alienated Smith and set La Russa at odds with the Cardinals fans and media. Despite sputtering early in the season, however, the Redbirds managed to climb into a tie for first in the NL Central at the All-Star break. On Labor Day weekend, St. Louis swept a three-game set with Houston and managed to win the Central with an 88–74 mark. It had been nine years since the team had guzzled any postseason champagne, making the title particularly sweet.

With the new league alignment, an additional playoff tier had been added. The three divisional champions and the team with the best second-place record (termed the wild-card) received postseason berths. The Redbirds romped through the first round—called the divisional series—sweeping the Western champion San Diego Padres in three and setting up a confrontation with Bobby Cox's Atlanta Braves, the World Series champions of 1995.

After dropping the opener to Atlanta ace John Smoltz, the Redbirds rebounded with three consecutive victories, placing them within a game of the World Series. From there, however, Smoltz, Greg Maddux, and Tom Glavine restored order for the Atlantans and the season was over. The final three games demonstrated Atlanta's superiority as they outscored St. Louis 32–1.

The following season opened with a six-game losing streak, and the Cardinals were never a factor in 1997 with a 73–89 campaign. There was a big story in 1997, however. Mark McGwire came over from Oakland to reunite with La Russa. Having blasted 34 homers in the Bay, he added 24 more for St. Louis, giving him 58 for the season. Those 58, added to the 52 he had hit for Oakland in 1996, made "Big Mac" the first player since Babe Ruth to clear the 50-home-run mark in consecutive seasons.

All of this set up 1998. The minor news was that the Cardinals were a mediocre 83–79, never in the NL Central chase. The major news was that 34-year-old Mark McGwire, from the outset of the season, went on a home-run rampage, one that ended with a record-breaking 70.

Forgotten amid the bedlam of 1998 is that McGwire slammed 65 more the following season, for a two-year total of 135 and a career total of 522. Another Cardinal, 24-year-old Fernando Tatis, hammered 34 more, making history by hitting two grand slams in a single inning off Dodgers hurler Chan Ho Park. The Cardinals, however, limped to a 75–86 record, and fans could be heard calling for La Russa's well-coifed scalp.

All was not good in Cardinal land, as the team closed the decade having posted four losing seasons over the previous six years. They had made only one postseason appearance that decade, a better showing than only the fifties and seventies, when they saw no postseason play. McGwire was old, La Russa was in trouble, and the new millennium was coming.

By the NUMBERS 351—Number of wins for Cardinals skipper Joe Torre during the nineties, the most of any Cardinals manager in that decade. He also had the best winning percentage, .498, out of those who managed at least 100 games.

A Race into History, But . . .

Few seasons have held sports fans' attention like that of 1998. It was the year of the home run—one never before seen in the century-plus history of major league baseball. And it started on Opening Day. In fact, the main-stage performer, Mark McGwire, hit one out in each of the first four games, equaling Willie Mays' 1971 record. The banging continued, earning McGwire player-of-the-month honors in April and May. By the All-Star break Big Mac had 37 circuit shots, tying Reggie Jackson's first-half record. McGwire thrived in baseball-crazy St. Louis and the non–designated hitter National League.

"It's amazing how many 1-2-3 innings you see over here," he remarked. "Those things never seem to happen in the American League. There is also so much more standing around in the American League. Here, you always feel into the game. It's just a better way to play the game." McGwire was really into the game. On August 19, with St. Louis visiting the Cubs in Wrigley, he had 47 home runs. Sammy Sosa, however, reached 48 with that day's homer. McGwire snapped back with a pair, and the two-man race was really on.

For McGwire the run at Roger Maris' record did not come without inordinate stress. As he closed in on the records of Ruth and Maris, he became curt and often less than cooperative with the media. "I don't think there's ever been another athlete to be singled out like I was singled out the last two months of the season," he remarked later.

He was most gracious toward the achievements of his predecessor, Roger Maris, who wore Cardinals Red back in the late sixties as a member of the championship teams of 1967 and 1968. "I touched Roger's bat and held it to my heart," he said. "My bat will lie next to his. I'm very proud of that."

McGwire was actually quite similar to Maris in that neither sought publicity. Maris was an introverted man, fiercely dedicated to his family and the game. Although he roomed with the philandering alcoholic Mantle, nary a word of scandal touched Roger Maris.

TRIVIA

Who led the Cardinals in home runs during the nineties?

Answers to the trivia questions are on pages 161–162.

Mantle, however, was far more popular with the media. He had been the center of attention in New York for many years, while Maris came from virtually nowhere to dominate the national stage. Once there in 1961, he avoided the media, answered in short phrases when he did speak, and became increasingly sullen as he approached Ruth's hallowed record. He found the pressure so torturous that some of his trademark crew cut began falling out. Regarded with respect and affection by teammates and managers throughout his career, Maris was a quality person who was simply ill-equipped to function in what was becoming a media age.

When it was over, he seemed more relieved than excited. "As a ballplayer, I would be delighted to do it again," Maris reflected. "As an individual, I doubt if I could possibly go through it again. They even asked for my autograph at mass."

The fans were just as enthralled with the 1998 home-run race. Big Mac and the fan-friendly Sosa captivated the baseball nation, one that needed a stimulant to recover from the ugliness of 1994. The two forged a friendship that prompted McGwire to remark, "Wouldn't it be great if we ended up tied? I think that would be beautiful."

McGwire, however, pushed on. By the first of September he broke Hack Wilson's NL record of 56 home runs in a single season. On September 5 he tied Ruth's 60, and two days later he caught up with Maris' 61. On September 8 he hit a ball 341 feet—good enough for number 62. In a classy gesture, McGwire credited Maris as an all-time great with whom he was honored to be associated, and he invited the Maris family to be on hand to honor the late slugger amid his own heroics. Pandemonium ruled as McGwire crossed the plate and entered history. He lifted his young son—a Cardinals batboy—in the air and hugged the Maris clan.

McGwire certainly had a feel for drama. The home run came at home, in front of a national television audience, and against Sammy Sosa and the Chicago Cubs. Sosa, always as gracious as McGwire, was not ready to relinquish 1998 to Big Mac. On the final Friday of the season he clouted his 66th home run in the Astrodome, pulling ahead in the derby. His reign was brief, however, as McGwire answered in St. Louis just 47 minutes later to pull even.

That was it for Sosa, but McGwire pressed on, smacking a pair in each of the Redbirds' final two games, to finish at 70.

McGwire's season numbers were, in a word, mammoth. In addition to his 70 home runs, he hit .299, scored 130 times, drove in 147, walked 162 times, and struck out in 155 at-bats. Those numbers were good enough for him to finish second in the MVP balloting. Sammy Sosa was first.

The euphoria of 1998 all but carried baseball over the threshold from national discontent to new levels of popularity. The McGwire-Sosa chase actually dwarfed the 73-home-run season just three years later by the less-than-popular Barry Bonds.

By 2004 more than McGwire's record had been broken—so had his reputation and those of other sluggers of the era, as rumors of widespread steroid use dominated sports journalism, much of the attention due to a book by former McGwire teammate Jose Canseco. On March 17, 2005, McGwire—an eminently decent man—offered some very emotional testimony before a congressional hearing on the use of steroids by athletes. Although McGwire would not answer questions as to whether he had bulked up on the substances, his words left little doubt in the hearers' minds that his majestic home-run performances had been aided by 'roids. Dave Sheinin of the *Washington Post* covered the inquiry and wrote, "The most extraordinary image of all was that of Mark McGwire, once the game's most celebrated slugger, but now the face of the steroid scandal, reduced to [a] shrunken, lonely, evasive figure whose testimony brought him to the verge of tears."

Anger poured out, even from former players. Hall of Fame pitcher Jim Bunning, a United States Senator, minced no words, stating, "When

History was made on September 8, 1998, when Mark McGwire hit home run number 62 against the Cubs, breaking one of baseball's most cherished records: Roger Maris' single-season record of 61 home runs, set in 1961.

I played with Henry Aaron, Willie Mays, and Ted Williams, they didn't put on 40 pounds . . . and they didn't hit more home runs in their late thirties than they did in their late twenties. What's happening in baseball is not natural, and it's not right." Bunning and others wanted the latter-day home-run records expunged from the books.

Commissioner Bud Selig ruled otherwise, keeping the records official, in part because there was simply no way to determine who used steroids and when. For those most enraged, the pro–McGwire and company argument suggests that players have sought competitive advantages throughout the game's history. Two Hall of Fame pitchers—Gaylord Perry and Don Sutton—admitted to doctoring the ball during their outstanding careers.

That notwithstanding, the steroid revelations were an unfortunate postscript to an otherwise uniquely exciting era.

A Century of Greatness

The 20th century was one of excellence for the St. Louis National League franchise. Not only did the Redbirds play the entire century in the National League, but they managed 15 pennants and nine World Series championships along the way. Fully 30 players who wore Cardinals Red during the century are in the Hall of Fame, 14 of whom played more games in Cardinals Red than in any other uniform.

The All-Century Cardinals Team

1B—Jim Bottomley

Bottomley, a Hall of Famer, played for the Cardinals in the twenties and won an MVP trophy in 1928 when he led the NL in home runs and RBIs. Twice he finished second in the NL in hitting, and six times Bottomley knocked in more than 100 runs for the Redbirds.

2B—Rogers Hornsby

Hornsby over Frisch is a very tough call. Like Frisch, Hornsby served as both player and manager. Though far less likable, Hornsby was simply a better player. He spent a dozen years in St. Louis, clearing the .400 barrier three times and winning six batting titles as a Cardinal. Twice he led the league in homers and four times in RBIs. Frisch, like Hornsby, snared an MVP, but he didn't get to St. Louis until he was 28.

3B—Ken Boyer

Boyer wins over the entertaining Pepper Martin. Bill James ranked Boyer as the 12th-best third baseman in history in his 2001 *Historical Baseball Abstract.* The seven-time All-Star hit 255 home runs for the Cardinals during his 11 seasons in St. Louis and took home an MVP trophy for his

Gabby Street (right) managed the Cardinals' "team of the century," the 1931 unit that won 101 games and the World Series and had five future Hall of Famers. Pictured with Street is Philadelphia Athletics manager Connie Mack.

performance on the 1964 championship team—a year in which Boyer led the league in RBIs. Martin was a base-stealing wizard—leading the NL three times—who made four All-Star teams and was a leader on the 1934 championship team. In 1933 he led the NL in runs scored with 122.

SS—Ozzie Smith

There is no contest here, as the Wizard of Oz—a first-ballot Hall of Famer—laps the field as the team's greatest shortstop. He made 15 All-Star teams (14 as a Cardinal) and won 13 Gold Gloves—11 in St. Louis. Three times Ozzie made the top 10 in number of times on base, and he was the toughest guy to strike out in 1986.

LF—Joe Medwick

Medwick won the Triple Crown and the MVP award in 1937, but he was a sensational player throughout his nine-year sojourn in St. Louis. A 10-time All-Star, he made the team six times wearing Cardinals Red. He hit over .300 all nine Redbirds years and drove in more than 100 runs six straight times.

CF—Lou Brock

Brock played the bulk of his St. Louis career in left field, in part because of the defensive brilliance of Curt Flood. Nevertheless, Brock was a center fielder early in his career, and he makes the all-century team at that position to make room for Medwick. After playing poorly as a Cub, Brock's caterpillar career grew into butterfly quality after arriving in St. Louis. The six-time All-Star led the league in stolen bases eight times, stealing 118 when he was 35 years old. Twice leading the league in runs scored, Brock placed in the top five in hits eight times. Behind Brock is Curt Flood, a three-time All-Star and seven-time Gold Glove winner, who placed in the top 10 in batting average five times.

RF—Stan Musial

The Man played right, left, and first base. His records are catalogued in the chapter on "the Man," but we can add here that although Musial won three MVPs, he finished second in the voting

TRIVIA

Has any Cardinal other than Stan Musial won the MVP award more than once?

Answers to the trivia questions are on pages 161–162.

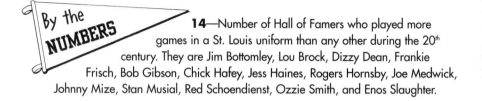

14—Number of Hall of Famers who played more games in a St. Louis uniform than any other during the 20ᵗʰ century. They are Jim Bottomley, Lou Brock, Dizzy Dean, Frankie Frisch, Bob Gibson, Chick Hafey, Jess Haines, Rogers Hornsby, Joe Medwick, Johnny Mize, Stan Musial, Red Schoendienst, Ozzie Smith, and Enos Slaughter.

on four other occasions. He was one of the top two players in the NL seven times. Though he never led the league in home runs, Stan hammered 475 of them, placing him in the top eight 11 times.

C—Ted Simmons

Bill James ranked Simmons 10ᵗʰ all-time among catchers. Simmons, who entered the majors at 18, was named to six All-Star teams in his 13 years in St. Louis, the same number of times he hit .300. He placed in the top 10 in hitting five of those years. A sturdy performer behind the plate, he placed in the top nine in games played three times, which was also the number of times he drove in more than 100 runs for the Cardinals. Tim McCarver, a favorite among many Cardinals rooters, was a better defensive catcher, played on three pennant winners, made two All-Star teams, and placed second in MVP balloting in 1967. (Simmons made the top 10 in MVP balloting three times.) McCarver topped Simmons in one category: age. The 11-year Cardinals veteran was in the majors at age 17.

P—Bob Gibson

Gibson's 251 wins earned him two Cy Young Awards and an MVP during his 17 years in Cardinals Red. The eight-time All-Star and nine-time Gold Glove winner was a big-game pitcher par excellence—winning two World Series MVPs. Four times he posted an ERA under 2.50, with an astounding 1.12 in 1968. Four times he led the NL in shutouts. A strikeout artist, "Hoot" placed in the top five in K's 10 different times. It would have been a different race for the pitcher's spot had Dizzy Dean remained healthy past his 27ᵗʰ birthday. Dean won 134 games in essentially six seasons as a Cardinal. He was a four-time All-Star and won an MVP trophy in 1934 as a member of the Gashouse Gang. In 1936 Dizzy led the league in complete games and saves and placed second in wins. He led the league in strikeouts four times, in innings pitched three times, and in shutouts twice.

It's a close call, but the nod goes to Gibson on the length of his sustained excellence.

TRIVIA

How many Cardinals pitchers have been named MVP?

Answers to the trivia questions are on pages 161–162.

Manager—Whitey Herzog
It's Whitey over the Redhead. Herzog—as GM and manager—remolded the Cardinals of the eighties. He won three pennants and a World Series after the Cardinals had not been in postseason play since 1968. His unique brand of baseball—speed, defense, and pitching—became known as Whitey Ball and became a major force during the eighties. Albert "Red" Schoendienst, as faithful a Redbird as has ever worn Cardinals Red, is a solid second. Schoendienst won more than 1,000 games in St. Louis and back-to-back pennants in 1967 and 1968. As for their records, Herzog posted a .530 winning percentage (822–728), while Schoendienst registered .522 (1,041–955). Billy Southworth had the best winning percentage of all at .642 (620–346), but he enjoyed his greatest success during the war years.

Other Awards
Team of the Century—1931 Cardinals
The 1931 club won 101 of 154 games, led by Hall of Famers Frankie Frisch, Jim Bottomley, Chick Hafey, Jesse Haines, and Burleigh Grimes. The team went on to beat Connie Mack's Philadelphia Athletics (107–45) in a seven-game World Series. Six pitchers won at least 11 games in 1931. The hurling sextuplets went an aggregate 88–48. The 1967 team also won 101 games (against 60 losses), and took a seven-game Series from Boston. That team had Hall of Famers Gibson, Brock, and Cepeda. The most dominant team of all was the 1942 club that won 106 and lost just 48 during the regular season and then took out the Yankees 4–1 in the Series. In 1943 and 1944, the Redbirds went on to back-to-back 105–49

DID YOU KNOW . . . That seven Cardinals MVPs are not in the Hall of Fame? Bob O'Farrell, Mort Cooper, Marty Marion, Ken Boyer, Joe Torre, Keith Hernandez, and Willie McGee were all MVPs but never made it to Cooperstown.

seasons, with the latter squad taking a 4–1 Series over the Browns. As great as those forties teams were, those were war years, seasons in which league talent was diminished.

Player of the Century—Stan Musial

Musial towers over all comers. An argument could be made for Ozzie Smith, Joe Medwick, Rogers Hornsby, Lou Brock, or Bob Gibson as runners-up: Smith for consistent excellence, Medwick for his run of greatness, Hornsby for his amazing performance in St. Louis, Brock also for his sustained contribution, and Gibson for his mound dominance. The choice is Gibby for number two and Hornsby number three. Hornsby was the greater player but spent a good chunk of his career with other teams.

CARDINALS SUPERLATIVES

Superlative	Player
Most Difficult	Rogers Hornsby
Nicest	Stan Musial
Most Entertaining	Dizzy Dean
Most Competitive	Bob Gibson
Greatest Leader	Frankie Frisch
Craziest Team	The 1934 Gashouse Gang

Out of the Gate in the New Millennium

More than the millennium was new in St. Louis in 2000. The team burst out of the gate in April 2000, posting a 17–8 mark. Cardinals fans were hoping this start was a sign of victories to come. After a 13–14 May, the Redbirds dialed it up once again, and by July 1 the team was roaring along with a 47–32 mark, certifiable contenders for not only the Central crown but the NL title as well.

A soft 11–15 July sent the Cards into August at 58–47, but the team turned the dog days into happy August nights, winning 17 of 28, and then finished the campaign with a monster 20–9 kick to go 95–67 for the season, a full 10 games in front of runner-up Cincinnati. St. Louis won the close ones (28–16 in one-run decisions) and the routs (31–16 in five-plus-run decisions). The team sported a powerful offense, scoring 887 runs and smacking 235 homers.

Jim Edmonds and Darryl Kile were the key off-season acquisitions. The Gold Glove center-field wizard, Edmonds, hammered a team-leading 42 home runs, knocked in 108, and scored 129 more. Kile, a refugee from the curse of Coors Field's bedeviling effect on pitchers, won 20 and lost only 9 in 34 starts for the team. Four other starters, who went 54–37 combined, helped push the Cardinals over the top.

It was a year not without adversity, however, as the team lost Mark McGwire to a chronic knee injury after he had already smacked 32 home runs. Cardinals GM Walt Jocketty, a front-office man who joined Redbirds ranks in the midnineties, stepped into the personnel fray with boldness. With Big Mac no longer protecting heavy-hitting Edmonds, and fearing an offensive collapse in now–hitter friendly (since its renovation) Busch, Jocketty snagged Will Clark from the Baltimore Orioles.

Clark hit a dozen home runs, knocked in 42 tallies, and hit .345 in just 51 games to close his career in a blaze of glory. It was the acquisitions of Clark, Edmonds, and Kile that brought Jocketty much-deserved Executive of the Year honors.

The Cardinals had depth. Five hitters launched at least 18 home runs, and five pitchers won at least 11 games, good omens for a successful postseason, one in which they would be matched against another 95–67 club, Bobby Cox's Atlanta wrecking crew. Realizing they would draw Greg Maddux and Tom Glavine in the first two games, concern was evident among Cardinals fans as their beloved Redbirds opened the division series in St. Louis. The Maddux-Glavine pair combined for 40 wins against just 18 losses during the campaign, with the team going just 55–49 in games in which the vaunted pair were not involved in the decision.

TRIVIA

Andy Benes has a brother who also pitched for the Cardinals in 2000. What is his name?

Answers to the trivia questions are on pages 161–162.

Tensions subsided as the Cards rocked mighty Maddux for six in the bottom of the first and rolled to a 7–5 victory, despite brilliant rookie southpaw Rick Ankiel's control problems. Glavine, a gritty postseason performer, was next, and the Cardinals knocked him out in the third, pounding him for seven runs en route to a 10–4 blowout win behind Kile. With all anxieties tranquilized, the team smacked Atlanta by a 7–1 margin in Game 3 to sweep the NLDS. Edmonds was all the rage in the NLDS, going 8 for 14, with six extra-base hits.

Hopes were soaring as the team awaited the outcome of the Mets-Giants encounter, which was won by the wild-card New Yorkers, three games to one. The Mets, however, took the first two games of their series with the Cardinals by 6–2 and 6–5 margins in St. Louis. Little did Cardinals fans realize that the unexpected radar problems that surfaced again in Game 2 for young Ankiel were an omen of what was to come— the end of the pitching career of a hurler with great promise. Andy Benes claimed Game 3 in New York, 8–2, bringing the Cards within one of squaring the NLCS.

It was not to be; the Mets swept the next two, 10–6 and 7–0, closing the door on what was still a rousing beginning to a new decade and millennium.

The 2001 season was even more entertaining, as the team struggled early, splitting 24 games evenly in April and barely keeping their heads above divisional water in a race against the Astros in the Central. The team put wheels under itself in May, going 17–11, only to sputter again in June, 11–16. Entering July at just 40–39, it looked like a return to the frustrations

Outfielder Ray Lankford makes a running catch over shortstop Edgar Renteria in action from Game 2 of the 2000 NLCS.

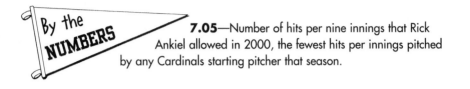

7.05—Number of hits per nine innings that Rick Ankiel allowed in 2000, the fewest hits per innings pitched by any Cardinals starting pitcher that season.

of the nineties. McGwire was in a virtual repeat of the previous season, hitting 29 home runs during an injury-plagued final year for Big Mac. With Clark retired, the team hoped 21-year-old rookie Albert Pujols could fill in the gap. He did. Pujols blasted 37 home runs and drove in 130 runs in an All-Star season, and the rest of the team managed to jell. Edmonds added 30 round-trippers and 110 RBIs, while J. D. Drew smacked 27 homers. On the mound, Matt Morris developed into an ace, going 22–8, while Kile added 16 more wins. The bullpen, however, was spotty, as no reliever was able to save more than 15 of the team's 38.

The team went on an out-and-out tear over the final two months of the season, winning 40 of their final 58 games. The slow start was costly, however, as the Redbirds had to run up a very steep hill in the second half, managing to tie Houston for the Central crown with a 93–69 mark. Because Houston won the season series between the two teams, 9–7, the Cardinals were dubbed the wild-card. Cardinals fans cared little about the lack of a divisional crown, because their beloved Redbirds were back in the postseason hunt.

Owing to their wild-card status the Cards would open on the road against the Arizona Diamondbacks. Facing Arizona was both good news and bad. It was good news because Arizona was a less-than-impressive 92–70 over the regular season. It was bad news because the team was led by two of the finest hurlers in the game, Randy Johnson and Curt Schilling. Reminiscent of the 1987 Twins, the D-backs could conceivably make it through the entire postseason successfully if the two pitchers could win each of their starts. This scenario was not out of the realm of possibility, as the two combined for 43 wins—nearly half the team total—against just 12 defeats in the regular season. The rest of the staff was 49–58. A short series actually favored the Arizona squad because they could pitch Johnson and Schilling in all but a few games, given the off days inserted in postseason play.

Matt Morris, however, was brilliant in the opener, holding the Diamondbacks to a single run. Unfortunately, Schilling was even better, as he shut out a Cardinals team that had averaged five runs per game, 1–0. The Redbirds managed just three hits off the right-handed ace.

It was Woody Williams against Randy Johnson in Game 2, in what figured to be a mismatch. Williams, who came over from San Diego in midseason, had a 15–9 regular season with a 4.05 ERA. Playing in St. Louis, however, he won 7 of those 15 against but one loss, with a puny 2.28 ERA. His counterpart, Johnson, had gone 21–6 for the campaign with a 2.49 ERA. Baseball, as former Cardinals player, announcer, and humorist Joe Garagiola put it, is a funny game, and the unexpected occurred in Arizona, as Williams won a 4–1 verdict, allowing just four hits over seven innings.

The series was now squared at one each, and the Cardinals held serve with the games moving to Busch. Especially heartening was that Schilling and Johnson would be on the sideline for Game 3, one in which La Russa sent Darryl Kile to the mound to gain the series lead against Miguel Batista. Kile had his stuff, and St. Louis held a 2–1 edge after six innings. The seventh, however, was a disaster, as the Diamondbacks exploded for four runs off three Redbirds hurlers and took the win 5–3 and the series lead.

La Russa gave rookie Bud Smith, who had appeared in only 16 regular-season games, the ball in the must-win Game 4. Bob Brenly countered Albie Lopez, a right-hander who had gone just 4–7 for Arizona (although he also pitched for Tampa Bay that year, going 9–19 overall) in 2001. La Russa's daring call paid off, as Smith permitted but one run over five innings, leaving with a 4–1 lead. The bullpen held up, and the Cardinals had a 2–2 split in the series. It was now down to an all-or-nothing Game 5 and a Morris-Schilling rematch. Both pitchers were equal to the task, as the score was knotted at 1 through eight innings in Arizona.

Dave Veres took over mound duties in the bottom of the ninth and was greeted by a ringing two-bagger by Matt Williams. Pinch runner Midre Cummings was pushed over to third on a sacrifice bunt by Damian Miller. Steve Kline intentionally walked pinch-hitter Greg Colbrunn. Then St. Louis got a

TRIVIA

Which speedy infielder led the Cardinals in triples in 2001?

Answers to the trivia questions are on pages 161–162.

DID YOU KNOW . . . That the biggest difference in the 2001 team compared to the 2000 team was pitching? In 2000 the Cardinals scored 887 runs and gave up 771. In 2001 the numbers were 814 (73 fewer runs scored) and 684 (87 fewer given up). The staff went from seventh to third in ERA.

terrific break as Cummings was tagged out while stealing on a busted squeeze. With two gone, all that stood in the way of an extra-inning tilt was light-hitting Tony Womack, who had already failed to execute the bunt. Womack, however, didn't cooperate, singling to left and driving in pinch runner Danny Bautista to win the series. The Diamondbacks would go on to take it all in 2001.

Two years into the new century and the Cardinals were truly out of the gate, winning 188 regular-season games, good for a pair of trips into the postseason, where the team had come just short of two NLCS appearances. Life was good baseball-wise for Cardinals fans, and they looked forward to it getting better.

Pushing On

The 2002 season started much as the previous campaign did, with the Cardinals limping through April with a 12–14 mark. An 18–10 May put them in contention with a 30–24 record. Fortunately, the pesky Astros were at 24–29, but the surprising Cincinnati Reds were 32–22. June was a step backward for the Cardinals, as they managed only 12 wins in their 24 games. Much, much worse, however, than any record was longtime Cardinals announcer Jack Buck's succumbing to cancer at age 77 on June 14, as the season roared along. Buck, who had taken over after Harry Caray's departure more than 30 years previous, was a truly beloved figure in St. Louis and a nationally recognized announcer. In fact, Buck actually preceded his predecessor Caray in being inducted into the broadcasters wing of the Baseball Hall of Fame. Moreover, it was the poetic Buck who stirred the St. Louis crowd to readiness when the baseball season resumed after September 11, 2001.

But Buck's death wasn't the worst of it.

Just four days later, ace pitcher Darryl Kile, in a Chicago hotel room, died in his sleep of undetected heart disease. Ironically, the veteran Kile had been among the only Redbirds pitchers to remain healthy early in the season. In addition, Kile was a natural team leader, one whom La Russa challenged to help get the team out of its early season psychological funk. The manager was now left with the task of getting his heartbroken team to push on in the face of its pain.

Amazingly, the skipper came across something Kile had written after the death of his own father. In the writing he noted that although it may seem cold, he had to continue to do his job and that his departed father would have expected nothing less of him. La Russa read Kile's thoughts to his team; with words that seemed to be coming from the grave, the team rallied, ripping through July with a 17–9 mark. Entering August with a promising 59–45 record, the team ground its way to 76–59 by September 1. Realizing the final month would tell the tale, La Russa pressed all the right buttons, steering his charges to a 21–6 finish and a 97–65 mark for the season, 13 games better than Houston for the division title.

The accomplishment brought him a well-deserved Manager of the Year award. To say La Russa pressed buttons is an understatement. No fewer than 21 pitchers won at least one game for the 2002 team. Moreover, the team's top two winners—Matt Morris and Jason Simontacchi—combined for just 28 triumphs. In addition, after Morris' 211 innings pitched, no other hurler threw more than 144. Jason Isringhausen, a Jocketty acquisition from Oakland, bolstered the relief staff, notching 32 of the squad's 42 saves.

Cardinals players in a moment of silence at Chicago's Wrigley Field to honor teammate Darryl Kile, who had passed away the day before, June 22, 2002. Kile was 33 years old.

By the
NUMBERS
.420—Jim Edmonds' on-base percentage in 2002, higher than Edgar Renteria's, Scott Rolen's, and Albert Pujols'.

Offensively, there was no sophomore jinx for Albert Pujols, as the young slugger drove home 127 runs, 44 more than shortstop Edgar Renteria and center fielder Jim Edmonds. The Cardinals' 175 home runs helped propel them to 787 runs scored for the season. Walt Jocketty also made another major contribution during the campaign, plucking hard-hitting third baseman Scott Rolen out of Philadelphia in July. Rolen managed 14 homers and 44 RBIs in just 55 games.

The divisional series figured to be high drama, a rematch of 2001 with the Schilling-Johnson D-backs, a team that had rung up 98 wins for the season. The matchup was clearly a matter of substantial concern to Cardinals rooters. Again, the first two games would be played in the desert.

Morris would open against the estimable Randy Johnson, who had gone an incredible 24–5 for the season. But the Redbirds were unimpressed with the Big Unit, rocking him for six runs in six innings. Morris was solid, and the Cardinals owned Game 1, 12–2. Lefty Chuck Finley was nominated to pitch in Game 2, facing a 23–7-on-the-season Curt Schilling. The game was a grinder, one in which J. D. Drew lifted St. Louis into an early 1–0 lead with a third-inning home run. The lead held up until the bottom of the eighth, when Pujols, having been moved to third at the outset of the inning, made an error on a ball hit by Greg Colbrunn, thus opening the gate for an Arizona run. In the ninth, Renteria led off with a single and was sacrificed to second on a bunt by Mike Matheny. Miguel Cairo then delivered Renteria with a single, and the Cards held on for a 2–1 win. The win put St. Louis up two games to none.

It was must-win time for the Diamondbacks at Busch in Game 3. Although Arizona jumped out to a 2–0 lead against Andy Benes in the third, the Cardinals would not be denied and rolled to a 6–3 win, completing the sweep and sending them on the NLCS against San Francisco.

The Giants, 95–66 during the campaign, jumped all over Morris in the opener at Busch, leading 6–1 after three innings. The Redbirds managed five runs in the last five innings, but they were not enough to

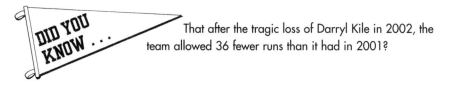

avoid a 9–6 defeat. Woody Williams drew Jason Schmidt in Game 2, and the Giants' right-hander was in top form, allowing just one run in seven and two-thirds innings. Williams pitched well, permitting just three runs in his six innings of work, but his performance fell short as the Giants cruised to an easy 4–1 win.

Time was running short for the Cardinals as they headed to San Francisco for Game 3. St. Louis, behind Finley, led 4–1 in the bottom of the fifth, only to have the Giants push over three tallies on a three-run circuit shot by Barry Bonds and tie the score at four. An Eli Marrero homer in the sixth, however, gave the Cardinals the margin necessary for a 5–4 win. La Russa tapped Benes for Game 4, and he responded with a strong performance, giving up just two runs and hurling into the sixth. The Cardinals jumped out to a two-run lead in the top of the first but could do no more, and the game was knotted at two after seven innings. Benito Santiago banged out a two-run homer in the eighth, and when the Cardinals could answer with just one in the ninth, the game went to San Francisco, 4–3, despite their being outhit 12–4 by the Cardinals, who now faced elimination.

Morris was brilliant in Game 5, shutting down the Giants through seven innings. His opponent, Kirk Rueter, however, matched him boot for boot, and the score was just 1–0 Cardinals going into the bottom of the eighth. San Francisco then pulled even on a sacrifice fly by Bonds and won it in the ninth on three straight singles. The series and the season were over. It was a tough finish, but the Cardinals team had accomplished much in the star-crossed campaign, leaving Cardinals fans with good reason to expect big things in 2003.

Another slow start put the 2003 Redbirds at 27–27 entering June. A 16–11 June put them at 43–38 and ready to make their run. July, however, proved disappointing (13–14), and a 16–12 August sent them into the

TRIVIA

Who was the only Cardinal to be named to both the 2001 and 2002 All-Star teams?

Answers to the trivia questions are on pages 161–162.

season's final month at just 72–64, although still in first place in the Central. Hit by injuries to Morris and closer Jason Isringhausen, the team stayed in a three-team race for the Central going into September. Losing four of five to the Cubs early in the month, however, sealed the team's fate, placing them third in the division with an 85–77 record. Dusty Baker's Cubs went on a September tear, while La Russa's charges managed only a .500 (13–13) finish, and the Redbirds were not to play in October.

The 2003 campaign belonged to young Albert Pujols, who won the batting title with a .359 mark and placed fourth in homers and RBIs with 43 and 124, respectively. He was the primary force behind the team's whopping 876 runs scored for the season. The team's woes, however, were on the mound, where Cardinals pitchers allowed a total of 796 runs.

With the injuries to Morris, who went just 11–8 on the year, and Isringhausen, who appeared in only 40 games, the pitching staff turned in a hefty 4.60 ERA, 11th in the National League. Woody Williams managed to win 18 games and Brett Tomko 13 more. Combined with Morris, the team's top three winners were 42–26 in the aggregate, but the rest of the staff was a mere 43–51. Overall the team yielded a whopping 148 runs more than they had in 2002. That run-per-game difference kept them out of October baseball.

Nonetheless, Redbirds fans had had a nice little four-year run since Y2K. The team had averaged more than 92 wins per season, won a pair of divisional crowns, made two trips to the NLCS, and been to the post-season three consecutive times.

DID YOU KNOW ... That, barring injury, Darryl Kile was on pace for a certain 200-win career and a probable 250-win career? He had 133 victories at the time of his death and had established a pace of more than 15 wins per season over the previous six years.

Return to Prominence

Which way would the team go in 2004? Would the Cardinals return to prominence or slide back into mediocrity? In fact, despite their fast start in the new century, little was expected of the Cardinals going into 2004, the midpoint of the decade. The Cubs and Astros looked to be the class of the Central, with the pitching-poor Redbirds doing their best to hit their way into contention, and everyone knowing that it wouldn't work.

Things went as expected in April, as the team managed a mediocre 12–11 month, one in which it allowed more than five runs per game while scoring at an only slightly better rate. Tony La Russa and Dave Duncan performed wonders with the pitching staff by May, as the team yielded more than one and a half runs fewer per game than in the opening month. That was the good news. The bad news was that the improvement contributed a still-noncontending 15–12 mark.

The dividends were reaped in June, however. The pitching held, and the Cardinals bats warmed up with the weather as the squad averaged 5.6 runs per game en route to a 19–9 mark. So at midseason the Redbirds stood at 46–32, clearly in the Central Division hunt. With the pitching getting even better, St. Louis went berserk in July and August, winning 41 and losing only 12. At 87–44, for the Cardinals the race was all but over, except they were on the inside rather than out. Eighteen more wins closed the books at an amazing 105–57, a 20-game improvement on 2003, and it came in a year in which little was expected of the team.

Through it all, the Redbirds offense did not disappoint, leading the NL with 855 runs. Scott Rolen, Jim Edmonds, and Albert Pujols were a three-cylinder scoring machine as the triumvirate drove in a total of 358 runs (five NL teams scored less than twice the crew's RBI number), while blasting 122 home runs.

Several Cardinals celebrate their 5–2 win in Game 7 of the 2004 NLCS over the Houston Astros.

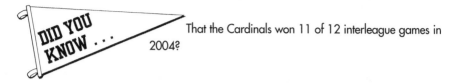

Moreover, the 659 runs allowed were also tops in the league, while the staff ERA of 3.75 was good for second in the National League. The defense was stellar, with Rolen, Edmonds, and catcher Mike Matheny taking home Gold Gloves.

Still, the eye-popping achievement of La Russa and company's efforts was the uptick in pitching. No fewer than four pitchers won at least 15 games for the Redbirds, while a fifth won 11 more. Matt Morris hurled a team-high 202 innings, while the number five man, Chris Carpenter, threw only 20 fewer innings. Morris, Carpenter, Williams, Jeff Suppan, and Jason Marquis were a combined 72–39. The rest of the staff stepped up as well, going 33–18.

St. Louis was averaging 95 wins per season in the new millennium, and La Russa—whose 2002 Manager of the Year citation was his fourth such award during his long career—was well in command.

It was postseason time again in Missouri, and the Cardinals opened at home against the Los Angeles Dodgers, a well-rounded team that had won the Western Division and was in the playoffs for the first time since the Tommy Lasorda era in 1996. A five-run explosion in the third, occurring after the first two Redbirds were retired, catapulted St. Louis and Woody Williams to an easy 8–3 win in the opener of the divisional series. The Cardinals erupted for 11 hits in Game 2, winning by an identical 8–3 score and jumping out to a 2–0 series advantage.

More than the scene shifted in Game 3, played at Dodger Stadium. Dodgers right-hander Jose Lima silenced the Cardinals' noisy bats on just five hits, as he and his mates rolled to a 4–0 victory. L.A. was one game away from evening the series, while the Redbirds were but a single win away from heading into the NLCS. Jeff Suppan took on Game 1 starter Odalis Perez in Game 4. Neither pitcher was particularly sharp early, as the score stood at 2–2 after three. Then, with one out in the fourth, Albert Pujols hammered a three-run homer and St. Louis was on the way to a 6–2 win and a date with the wild-card-winning Houston Astros, their Central Division rivals.

Williams got the nod against young Brandon Backe in the opener. Williams struggled, and at the halfway point, the Astros led, 4–2. In the bottom of the fifth, the Cardinals put two over the plate to tie the score, and then in the sixth, the Redbirds erupted for six runs on five hits, making the score 10–4. The 'Stros picked up three more, but the final tally was 10–7, St. Louis.

TRIVIA

Who led the Cardinals in RBIs in 2004?

Answers to the trivia questions are on pages 161–162.

Up 1–0 in the series and with ace Matt Morris on the mound at home against 29-year-old Pete Munro—not one of Houston's strongest pitchers in 2004—the NLCS appeared well in the Cardinals' hands. Morris, however, didn't have it and St. Louis found itself trailing 3–0 after four and a half. With two outs and one on in the bottom of the fifth, the Cardinals' scoring machine kicked in, as homers by Larry Walker and Scott Rolen contributed to a four-run uprising. By the seventh, however, Houston had tied it at four and was looking to get out of St. Louis with a 1–1 series split. It wasn't to be, as Pujols and Rolen went the distance in the eighth and the Cardinals had Game 2, 6–4.

Houston trotted out the inimitable Roger Clemens at home in Game 3, while La Russa nominated Jeff Suppan. Suppan threw six innings, shutting out the Astros in five of them. The problem was that in the other inning—the first—Houston hit him for three runs, all Clemens and his mates needed to win by a 5–2 score. Jason Marquis took the hill against Astros 20-game-winner Roy Oswalt in Game 4. With Oswalt figuring to hold down the Cardinals offense, Marquis needed to pitch a gem. But neither pitcher was on top of his game, and the score was knotted at five after six innings. A Carlos Beltran homer in the seventh was the difference, and the series was squared at two each.

Whoever won Game 5 would be up 3–2 and become prohibitive favorites to go to the World Series. Brandon Backe took the mound for Houston, while Woody Williams hurled for St. Louis. Backe got through the first unscathed, then the second, third, and fourth as well. Williams, however, was equal to the task, and the game was scoreless through four.

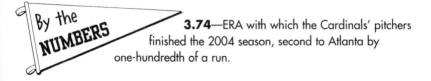

3.74—ERA with which the Cardinals' pitchers finished the 2004 season, second to Atlanta by one-hundredth of a run.

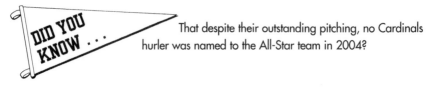

The fifth was a blank for both teams, as were the sixth and seventh. Each pitcher had yielded only one hit in what had become a 0–0 nail-biter for the series advantage. Backe chucked another scoreless frame in the eighth, while Jason Isringhausen replaced the brilliant Williams and did the same for the Redbirds.

When St. Louis failed to score in the ninth off reliever Brad Lidge, anxieties rose, and for good reason. With two on and one out, Astros second baseman Jeff Kent hit an Isringhausen offering out of Minute Maid Park and the Astros were within one game of ending the Cardinals' season.

Game 6 pitted Munro against Matt Morris, with the Redbirds hoping they would enjoy the same good fortune versus Munro as they had in Game 2. They did and led 4–2 after three innings. But Houston manager Phil Garner was not out of mound options. He turned to Chad Qualls and Dan Wheeler, and the pair—from the third inning on—responded with five and two-thirds innings of shutout ball. When the Astros picked up a run in the ninth on a Jeff Bagwell RBI single off Isringhausen, the game was tied at four. The taut drama then went on with neither team threatening in the tenth or eleventh, and the game entered the twelfth with the Houston bench so empty that pitcher Brandon Backe was brought in to pinch hit for Brad Lidge. He struck out for a three-up, three-down frame. Dan Miceli would face the meat of the Cardinals order in the twelfth. He opened by walking Pujols, bringing the dangerous Scott Rolen to the plate. Rolen, however, popped out. With the threat eased somewhat, Jim Edmonds strode to the plate, picked out an attractive Miceli offering, and drove it out of Busch for a dramatic 12-inning, 6–4 Redbirds triumph. The NLCS was locked at three games each.

The Cardinals had survived, but prospects were none too bright, as they would face Clemens in the deciding tussle, with Suppan taking the hill for St. Louis and needing to pitch the game of his life. Suppan was outstanding, allowing just two runs in his six innings of work. Unfortunately, the matchless Clemens held a 2–1 lead heading into the bottom of the sixth. Roger Cedeno then led off with a single, batting for Suppan. When

Renteria bunted him over to second, things looked better for St. Louis, but Larry Walker grounded out and Clemens was within a single out of quelling the threat. Albert Pujols doubled home Cedeno to tie the score, then Scott Rolen did an Edmonds of the game before, hitting a two-run

TRIVIA

Which NL team was the only one against which the Cardinals had a losing regular-season record in 2004?

Answers to the trivia questions are on pages 161–162.

shot, and the Cardinals were up 4–2 with just three innings left. Kiko Calero, Julian Tavarez, and Isringhausen each pitched a scoreless inning, and the Cardinals were heading to the World Series after a come-from-behind 5–2 victory.

It was the St. Louis Cardinals versus the wild-card Boston Red Sox in a World Series opening in Boston on October 23. The Red Sox jumped out to a 7–2 advantage through three innings in Game 1, but by the seventh the score was tied. The Bosox added a pair in the bottom of the frame, but the Cardinals answered with two of their own in the top of the eighth to make it a 9–9 slugfest. Boston then put two more over in the bottom of the inning, ending the scoring in the 24-hit encounter.

Curt Schilling, then wearing a Red Sox uniform, chilled the St. Louis bats with a 6–2 win in Game 2. Two days later Pedro Martinez put down the Cardinals at Busch, 4–1, and even the most ardent of Redbirds fans had their doubts, as their heroes' bats seemed dead. A day later Derek Lowe went seven innings, as the Red Sox completed the sweep with a 3–0 triumph, winning their first World Series in 86 years. Despite the bitter Series loss, St. Louis won 112 games in 2004, the most ever by a Cardinals team—and in a year in which no one expected them to be much of a factor.

It was a glorious start for the St. Louis Cardinals, halfway through the first decade of the 21st century. Five straight winning seasons, four trips to the playoffs, and yet another pennant continued to add to the luster of Cardinal Red.

Looking Back on La Russa's Journey to Managerial Success

In 1979 the Chicago White Sox were languishing in the backwaters of the American League West under the tutelage of player/manager Don Kessinger. Just two years previous the Pale Hose won 90 games under Bob Lemon. Then, after a slow start the following season, owner Bill Veeck made what was at the time a bold move. He replaced Lemon with Larry Doby, making Doby only the second African-American manager up to that time.

Upon closer examination, Doby was not an altogether surprising choice. He was the first black player in the American League, desegregating the Cleveland Indians, owned by none other than Veeck. The 1978 season turned out to be a lost year for the Sox, and Veeck, hoping to cash in on Kessinger's celebrity in Chicago and the still-novel concept of the player/manager, tapped the former Cubs great to manage on the Windy City's Southside. It was an ill-fated experiment. The team did not respond with wins, and Kessinger felt uncomfortable in the role, resigning after 106 games.

Who would be next? The answer was a 34-year-old former bonus-baby bust turned minor league manager, Anthony Joseph La Russa Jr. Veeck, a maverick intellectual, liked the budding young lawyer, instructing him to complete his legal preparation during the off-season. Despite finding favor with his employer, La Russa was a manager at risk. The professional mortality rate for first-time managers is abnormally high because they often take over poor teams with little cash to invest in talent. When things don't turn around quickly they are hastily dispatched. In short, La Russa did not have much time. He used what he had well, spurring the laggardly White Sox to a 27–27

DID YOU KNOW . . . That although La Russa never appeared in a major league game for the organization, the Cardinals were the last team to hold his contract as a player?

record for the balance of the 1979 season. The following season, the Sox managed to go just 70–90. Despite the unhappy record, La Russa's grip on the managerial job appeared safe given the esteem in which Veeck held him. The cash-strapped Veeck, however, rocked that security by selling his interests in the Chicago White Sox to Jerry Reinsdorf at the conclusion of the season.

Reinsdorf's desire to reshape the team, however, did not extend to the baseball brain trust, as he retained GM Rollie Hemond and the dugout skipper, La Russa. Two winning seasons followed, and by 1983 the White Sox flowered into a baseball power, winning the AL West by 20 games, much due to the wizardry of La Russa and his pitching coach and alter ego Dave Duncan in their handling of the Sox pitching staff.

Despite the team's success, and the incisive leadership of the scholarly La Russa, the manager simply did not catch on in blue-collar Chicago. He seemed uptight, defensive, humorless, and had a tendency to take himself and his decisions much too seriously. Players, for the most part, have not seen him that way. In fact, many cite La Russa as decidedly the best manager for whom they have played, highlighting the skipper's player relations and his efforts to put them in situations in which they can be successful.

The 1983 season proved a high point, as the Sox sputtered over the next two seasons, pushing Reinsdorf to make a bizarre move of his own. He sacked Hemond and installed popular play-by-play announcer Ken "Hawk" Harrelson in the GM role. The move proved calamitous, and Harrelson was out after one year. During the Hawk's tenure, however, La Russa—26–38

By the NUMBERS 11—Number of times a La Russa team has made the playoffs.

Tony La Russa in the dugout during Game 7 of the NLCS against the Braves in 1996.

through 64 games and totally out of synch with the cowboy's zany and often illogical baseball style—was sent packing.

It was 1986, and La Russa, who had managed since late 1979, was a free agent. It didn't take long for his phone to ring with Oakland on the other end

TRIVIA

La Russa appeared in 132 games as a player. What was his primary defensive position?

Answers to the trivia questions are on pages 161–162.

of the line, urging him to take over the A's. With that, La Russa was off to northern California, finishing the 1986 campaign with a 45–34 record as the new Oakland manager. La Russa, Duncan, and company swiftly made their presence felt in the Bay Area. After going 81–81 in 1987, the A's began a three-year run at the top of the American League, posting a 104–58 mark in 1988. The following year La Russa had his World Series ring as the A's took out the Giants in the 1989 fall classic.

By 1995 things had soured in the bay, as the team, lacking financial muscle, was unable to retain key players and sign able replacements. La Russa, after suffering through three consecutive losing seasons, left at the end of the 1995 season. An established manager and much in demand, La Russa had the luxury of waiting for the right opportunity to return to the dugout. He didn't wait long, signing with the Cardinals for the 1996 campaign.

The first four years in St. Louis were rocky. An 88–74 mark and first-place finish in the 1996 NL Central was followed by a 73–89 season the next year. After rebounding to an 83–79 campaign in 1998, the team slipped back to 75–86 in 1999. The taciturn La Russa found himself no more popular than he had been in Chicago more than a decade earlier, and the run in Oakland now appeared to be more the result of effective managing than the presence of superstar players. Cardinals fans longed for the return of Whitey Ball if not Whitey, himself.

The new millennium, however, brought different fortunes for La Russa and the Cardinals. The team went on a 575–397 six-year tear, and La Russa came to be regarded as one of the giants of the dugout, one of just nine managers to win in excess of 2,000 games.

La Russa's humorlessness masks a quiet intensity, a serious, conscientious approach to baseball, one characterized by a preparation for each game that is second to none. A student of the computer printout, with note cards in his pocket during games, La Russa sees the game as one of matchups, and his objective is to gain the edge in as many of these matchups as possible. Over the years knowledgeable baseball followers have come to see the introverted La Russa less as an aloof elitist and more as a careful and caring student of the game, one who respects and loves the game itself, and those who play it.

Prince Albert

He was born on January 16, 1980, in Santo Domingo of the Dominican Republic, and his name is Jose Alberto Pujols. In five short years, however, he has gathered a number of other names as well, including Phat Albert, the Machine, El Hombre, and Prince Albert, all references to this 6'3", 210-pound young man's incredible offensive prowess on the baseball diamond.

No Cardinal since Stan Musial has taken the game by greater storm than Albert Pujols, although unlike Musial, who began as a pitcher, many saw the young Dominican as a budding superstar at the plate when he was drafted in 1999. That, however, was in the United States. Few who knew Albert's origins would even imagine he would be healthy and strong and playing baseball at all, given the extreme poverty in which he grew up in Santo Domingo. The Pujols family was so poor that they lived in a communal setting and relied on government assistance to survive. Reared by a religiously devout grandmother, young Alberto learned faith and discipline and has held tightly to both throughout his life.

Baseball, however, was in his genes, as his usually absent father, Bienvenido, was known as one of the Dominican Republic's greatest pitchers of his time. By age 16, young Pujols joined other members of his family in New York City. Life in New York was traumatic as well as expensive. Albert, while on an errand once, witnessed a man being shot to death. His incredible grandmother stepped in and moved the family to Independence, Missouri, where a community of Dominicans already had settled.

It was in Missouri that Albert really cut his teeth on baseball. He saw a major league game between the Royals and the then California Angels. He also got his chance to play organized baseball in high school and the

American Legion. Realizing the value of speaking English and believing it would help him actualize his dream of playing in the major leagues, the highly motivated Pujols studied English with a tutor.

Albert was a baseball terror at Fort Osage High School, where he hit over .500 with 11 homers in his first season, including one round-tripper that went more than 450 feet. By the end of his sophomore year, Pujols had been named All-State twice and was piquing the interest of professional scouts. An excellent and highly motivated student, Pujols moved on to Maple Woods Community College where the shortstop with prodigious power helped his team to the Junior College World Series.

That the Cardinals drafted Pujols as a 19-year-old evidenced his strength and raw potential; however, they waited until the 13th round to do so and offered the youngster just $10,000 to sign. A disappointed Pujols turned them down and played in a summer league, excelling beyond expectations. When the Cardinals added $50,000 to their original offer, Pujols accepted and headed for Arizona for instructional baseball, where he learned to play third base.

Albert Pujols represents the future of the Cardinals. A rookie in 2001, he hit 160 home runs before the age of 25, collected more than 500 RBIs, and batted .333.

His hard work, discipline, and sturdy values—rooted in his Christian faith—propelled him up baseball's chain, and by Opening Day 2001, the 21-year-old was in the Cardinals' starting lineup. He was playing for more than just himself and his ego. On January 1, 2000, the then 19-year-old married his girlfriend Deidre, a young woman who had a daughter with Down syndrome.

The young family man simply tore into major league baseball, being named Rookie of the Month in April and May and landing on the National League All-Star team. By season's end Pujols had hit 37 home runs and 47 doubles and drove home 130 runs while scoring 112 more. That in addition to a .329 average made him a unanimous selection as Rookie of the Year, as well as his team's Triple Crown winner. He also managed to play four positions: left field, right field, and first and third bases.

Since then Pujols has been simply unrelenting. In 2002 he had another .300 season (.314), 34 home runs, 127 RBIs, and 118 runs scored. The following year, one in which Albert suffered what many thought might be a season-ending elbow injury, Pujols delivered 43 more homers, along with 124 RBIs, 137 runs scored, and a .359 batting average. In 2004 it was 46 homers, 123 RBIs, 133 runs scored, and a .331 hitting mark. In his fifth season there appeared to be simply no end in sight, as Pujols hit .330 with 41 homers, 117 RBIs, and 129 runs scored.

Despite his incredible power—201 home runs in five seasons—Pujols is not simply a burly slugger. He is a line-drive hitter who hits to all fields and simply lifts the ball out of the park on a regular basis. What is perhaps even more amazing is that he never struck out even 100 times in any of his first five seasons, yet he averaged 80 walks per year. He is one of those rare slugging superstars whose walk totals exceed his strikeouts.

Clearly the league's best player in 2005, Pujols finished in the top five in MVP voting in each of his first four years. His .500 average and four home runs made him the 2004 NLCS MVP in the high-drama battle with Houston.

To put Pujols' accomplishments in perspective, consider this: he has never hit less than .314, hit fewer than 34 home runs, driven in less than 117 runs, or scored less than 112 runs in any of his first five seasons; his high-water marks are a .359 average, 46 home runs, 130 RBIs, and 137 runs.

Albert by the Numbers

When it comes to the truly important measures of offensive greatness, Pujols has already taken his place among the greatest players of the game. Below are his rankings, through 2005, in four major categories: on-base percentage, slugging percentage, OPS (on-base plus slugging percentage), and batting average.

On-Base Percentage

1.	Barry Bonds	.442
2.	Todd Helton	.433
3.	Frank Thomas	.427
4.	Albert Pujols	.416*t*
	Lance Berkman	.416*t*

Slugging Percentage

1.	Albert Pujols	.621
2.	Barry Bonds	.611
3.	Todd Helton	.607
4.	Manny Ramirez	.599
5.	Vladimir Guerrero	.587

OPS

1.	Barry Bonds	1.053
2.	Todd Helton	1.040
3.	Albert Pujols	1.037
4.	Manny Ramirez	1.008
5.	Frank Thomas	.995

Batting Average

1.	Todd Helton	.337
2.	Albert Pujols	.332
3.	Ichiro Suzuki	.332
4.	Vladimir Guerrero	.324
5.	Nomar Garciaparra	.320

Albert and Stan Side by Side

Pujols is often compared to Stan Musial, and for good reason. No Cardinal since Musial has even approached the Man's numbers—until now. Below is a table comparing Musial's and Pujols' totals at age 25.

	AB	R	H	2B	HR	XBH	RBI	BB	BA
Pujols	2,954	629	982	227	201	439	621	401	.332
Musial	2,323	439	812	185	52	301	357	289	.350

Other than batting average, an area in which Musial excelled, Pujols is well ahead of the Man's pace at age 25, particularly in the power stats—doubles, homers, extra-base hits, and runs batted in.

Taking a longer view, Pujols is on pace to have more than 400 home runs, 1,300 RBIs, 1,300 runs, 500 doubles, and 2,000 hits by the time he is just 31 years old. Again, that is a Stan-the-Man pace. In fact, it is better, as the table below indicates.

	R	H	2B	HR	RBI
Pujols at 31 (projected)	1,300	2,000	500	400	1,300
Musial at 31	1,104	2,023	415	227	1,149

The table below contains Musial's career numbers in the same five categories. On the second line are the number of runs, hits, doubles, homers, and RBIs Pujols would need after age 31 should he reach the rather reasonable projection in the table above.

	R	H	2B	HR	RBI
Musial (career)	1,949	3,630	729	475	1,951
Needed by Pujols after age 31	649	1,630	229	75	651

Nothing is certain; therefore, it is always dangerous to project too far into the future. Musial's numbers are enormous and will be difficult to equal. What we do know, however, is that Pujols is on a pace to exceed most—if not all—of them.

Ranking with the Greats at 25

Below is how Pujols ranked in six categories at 25 years old, compared to all other major leaguers at the same age.

Note that Pujols is the only active player to make both the OPS and the doubles lists. In fact, only one other active player—Alex Rodriguez—made even one of the lists. The others are all Hall of Fame greats.

OPS

1.	Ted Williams	1.123
2.	Babe Ruth	1.101
3.	Jimmie Foxx	1.073
4.	Lou Gehrig	1.069
5.	Albert Pujols	1.037

Doubles

1.	Joe Medwick	258
2.	Ty Cobb	230
3.	Alex Rodriguez	228
4.	Albert Pujols	227
5.	Mel Ott	224

Pujols' power numbers also truly stack up against those of the greats of the game. Every retired player on each list is in the Hall of Fame.

Extra-Base Hits

1.	Jimmie Foxx	484
2.	Alex Rodriguez	483
3.	Mel Ott	476
4.	Albert Pujols	439
5.	Joe Medwick	433

Home Runs

1.	Alex Rodriguez	241
2.	Jimmie Foxx	222 *t*
	Eddie Mathews	222 *t*
4.	Mel Ott	211
5.	Mickey Mantle	207
6.	Frank Robinson	202
7.	Albert Pujols	201

Runs created is one of the most popular of baseball's new statistics. RC, derived from a complex formula, expresses the total number of runs a player actually generated. As such, it is a highly important statistic. Here again, Pujols joins the most elite of company.

Runs Created

1.	Jimmie Foxx	928
2.	Mel Ott	902
3.	Mickey Mantle	849
4.	Ty Cobb	835
5.	Alex Rodriguez	811
6.	Albert Pujols	757

Cardinals fans who remember Stan the Man will never forget him—so large a shadow did he cast with his heroics and personal class from 1941 to 1963 and into retirement. Few ever expected to see anyone like him again, on or off the field.

They may be wrong. Indeed, Jose Alberto Pujols is on pace to be the Man of the new millennium.

Continued Dominance

The 2005 season arrived with expectations soaring in the city of the arch. Despite the bitterness of the four-game World Series sweep by the almost-miraculous Red Sox in 2004, the Cardinals' campaign that year had generated 112 wins, including postseason play, against just 65 losses. Moreover, given their 85 wins in 2003—the *worst* performance in the new millennium—the Cardinals were now an established force, in fact *the* established force in the National League.

Despite losing Edgar Renteria and Mike Matheny in the off-season, fans looked forward with unbridled anticipation to the 2005 heroics of Pujols, Rolen, Edmonds, Morris, Carpenter, Isringhausen, and company, all under the discerning control of manager Tony La Russa and GM wizard Walt Jocketty. La Russa loved for his teams to get out of the gate quickly, establishing an early edge over the scrum of opponents, and his team did not disappoint. By the end of April the 15–7 Redbirds were perched three and a half games ahead of the second-place Cubs.

By the close of May the lead was six and a half, as the Cardinals had stretched their record to 33–18, the best mark in the NL and second overall to only the surprising White Sox. On July 4, often considered the halfway milestone in the annual season marathon, the race appeared all but over in the NL Central. St. Louis, 52–30, towered over the runner-up Cubs by 11½ games. The team's .634 percentage was easily the best in the NL.

Despite the joyous beginning, all was not well in Cardinal land. Scott Rolen was injured early and was gone for the season after appearing in only 56 games, pressing a comparatively lighter-hitting Abraham Nunez into handling much of the third-base duties. Aging Larry Walker was in and out of the lineup and contemplating retirement at season's end, as

Chris Carpenter won 21 games for the Cardinals in 2005. He is shown here beating the Astros' Roger Clemens on July 17, 3–0, to pick up win number 14.

his body was wearing down after a long career of all-out play. Moreover, bullpen ace Jason Isringhausen fought through some maladies as well. Nonetheless, the ever-vigilant La Russa—exploiting every edge available— had his team in first by 13½ games on September 1, sporting a major league–best 85–49 mark. With regulars resting in order to ready the squad for a postseason run, the Cardinals won 15 of their final 28 games to finish at 100–62 for the season. The team's continued dominance was in clear evidence, as St. Louis had won 205 regular-season games over the previous two seasons, easily the best in the majors.

If there had been any doubts as to the superstardom of Albert Pujols prior to 2005, he erased them in this banner season, all but carrying the offensive load on his back. Playing in 161 games, he notched a .330 average and fashioned 41 homers and 117 RBIs. Only one other Cardinal had more than 21 home runs and 61 RBIs (Jim Edmonds with 29 and 89, respectively).

Several other players made substantial contributions as well. David Eckstein ably filled the shortstop hole and scored 90 runs off a .363 on-base percentage. Veteran Mark Grudzielanek took over at second base for 137 games and hit .294. Overall the team tallied a third-best 805 runs, just 15 fewer than league-leading Cincinnati.

TRIVIA

Which popular baseball book, published in 2005, focused on manager Tony La Russa?

Answers to the trivia questions are on pages 161–162.

The pitching, especially the starting pitching, was magnificent. Under the watchful eye of Dave Duncan, Chris Carpenter, Mark Mulder, Jeff Suppan, Matt Morris, and Jason Marquis started 160 of the team's 162 contests. The aggregate turned in an 80–47 mark. Carpenter turned in an off-the-chart season, going 21–5 with a 2.83 ERA, while Mulder and Suppan each won 16. Julian Tavarez, Ray King, and Al Reyes were bullpen workhorses, appearing in a combined 216 games, while Isringhausen managed to convert 39 of 43 save opportunities. As a team, St. Louis led all of baseball with a 3.49 team ERA.

The 2005 campaign was somewhat bizarre. On one hand, the Cardinals ran away with the Central flag, playing well above .600 ball throughout the season. On the other hand, the San Diego Padres won the West with a mere 82–80 mark. In the middle of the muddle was Atlanta,

By the NUMBERS

7—Number of losing records Tony La Russa has posted in the 25 full seasons he has managed through 2005. He has 17 winning season and one .500 season.

which won the East with 90 victories. Houston and Philadelphia were in an all-out battle for the wild-card slot, with Houston having 89 wins and Phillies 88. Because Houston was in the Central, the Cardinals opened their postseason pilgrimage in a best-of-three series versus San Diego.

On the face of it, the divisional series figured to be easy, with the Cards facing a team they had outplayed by fully 18 games. The Padres' strength, however, was their pitching, and all they would need was two starters and their bullpen turning in some strong performances to sneak past the Cards in a short best-of-three confrontation. The situation was intensified by the nothing-to-gain-and-everything-to-lose pressure under which the Cardinals were playing—the baseball world expecting no less than a return trip to the Series and probably a triumph.

Waiting for St. Louis in the opener was Padres ace Jake Peavy, as good a starter as could stand on an NL mound. Peavy, despite some injuries, had started 30 games, tossed three shutouts, and registered a sparkling 2.88 ERA behind a 13–7 log. La Russa countered with 21-game-winner Chris Carpenter. It looked like a guaranteed low-scoring struggle, the type in which a San Diego victory was more than possible. It wasn't. Unbeknownst to the baseball public, Peavy suffered from a rib injury and was wholly ineffective, parting with eight runs in just four-plus innings. Peavy was shut down for the season after the contest. Edmonds hit a solo shot off the Padres pitcher in the first, and Reggie Sanders piled on with a grand slam in the fifth to put the game out of reach. Meanwhile, Carpenter tossed six shutout frames as the Cardinals took the opener by an 8–5 margin. There were some anxious moments, however, as the Padres rallied for three in the ninth and ended the game with the bases loaded.

In Game 2, lefty Mark Mulder faced off against reinvigorated veteran Pedro Astacio. Astacio, once a tremendous hurler for the Dodgers, had in recent years been toiling in baseball's backwaters, but he had returned to win four of six decisions for San Diego with a solid 3.17 ERA. No one knew quite what to expect from the seasoned right-hander. After two

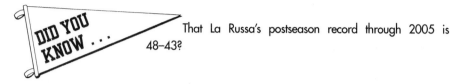

DID YOU KNOW . . . That La Russa's postseason record through 2005 is 48–43?

scoreless innings, however, the Redbirds' bats went to work on Astacio in the next two frames, giving St. Louis a 4–0 lead after four. The team coasted to a comfortable 6–2 win.

With the series 2–0, the Cards headed west, hoping to wrap it up in three. The year before, it had taken an extra game when the Dodgers' Jose Lima shut them out after the Cardinals had won the opening pair in St. Louis. It would be veteran ace Matt Morris against Woody Williams. Williams, a crafty right-hander, gave the Cards reason for concern because—having been a Redbird in recent years—he was thoroughly familiar with how to pitch to his former mates. The concern was misplaced, however, as the Cardinals' bats clubbed Williams for five runs in the first two innings en route to an easy, series-clinching 7–4 win.

Meanwhile, Houston was taking down Atlanta in four, finishing the series with an 18-inning marathon win at Minute Maid, so the NLCS was a reprise of 2004's seven-game nail-biter in which each team won all its home games, and therefore, the Cardinals prevailed. Houston would be formidable as they sported three of the game's best hurlers: Andy Pettitte, Roy Oswalt, and the inimitable Roger Clemens.

The series opened in St. Louis with Chris Carpenter going against Andy Pettitte. It figured to be a tight matchup, because as brilliant as Carpenter was, Pettitte had carved out a reputation for winning the big games. In fact, with 14, he was only one behind Atlanta's John Smoltz for the postseason win record and was 5–0 in his last six second-round starts. This was a game the Cardinals needed but one in which they could not be too confident.

Redbirds fans were delirious when, in the first inning, Reggie Sanders, who had already driven in 10 runs in the NLDS, ripped a 445-foot two-run homer to put the hometown favorites up, 2–0. Carpenter was splendid as his mates padded the lead until it became 5–0 by the end of the fifth. As it was, Carpenter threw eight strong innings, and the Cardinals rolled to a 5–3 win.

Mark Mulder took the mound in Game 2, this time against the Astros' 20-game-winner Roy Oswalt. Young Chris Burke bashed a three-bagger in the second and scored on a passed ball, putting Houston up, 1–0. The Astros added another tally in the fifth, and that was all they needed— Oswalt shocked the Cardinals' bats in a 4–1 win. The series was tied, but even worse, La Russa was headed for Texas and facing the possibility of having to play without slugger Reggie Sanders, who left the game with a lower-back sprain after crashing to the turf near the wall in pursuit of a shot off the bat of Houston's Adam Everett. In addition, the bullpen was missing key right-hander Al Reyes, and lefty Ray King was not available either.

As if those woes were not enough, Astros skipper Phil Garner had none other than Roger Clemens ready for the Redbirds upon their arrival in the Lone Star state. La Russa would counter with Matt Morris, who had averaged just short of 16 wins per season over the past five campaigns in St. Louis. Both pitchers were on their game, as neither team scored in the first three innings. In the bottom of the fourth, however, Mike Lamb hit a two-run homer and Houston was up, 2–0. The Cardinals chipped away against Clemens, thought to have a tender hamstring, with a run in the fifth and another an inning later to tie the score.

Then came the dreaded bottom of the sixth. The Astros took the lead when a one-out single by Jason Lane delivered Mike Lamb, who had doubled. Brad Ausmus then singled to right, where Larry Walker fired a throw to third

TRIVIA

Which Cardinals left-hander led the pitching staff in appearances in 2005?

Answers to the trivia questions are on pages 161–162.

baseman Abraham Nunez. Nunez collided with Lane, injuring his knee, and was removed for Hector Luna. The very next hitter, Adam Everett, hit a bounder to third. Luna fielded it cleanly but threw it over catcher Yadier Molina's reach and Houston was up, 4–2. The Cardinals managed a ninth-inning run off Brad Lidge, their first off Lidge since May 29, 2003, but it was not enough. Houston held the series lead.

It would be young Brandon Backe against veteran Jeff Suppan in Game 4. Both were brilliant. With a single run by each team in the fourth, the game stood at 1–1 through five. Backe gave way to Mike Gallo with two outs in the sixth, as the Cardinals failed to score again. Jason Marquis took over in the sixth for St. Louis and shut down the 'Stros once again. After a scoreless top of the seventh, Houston mounted a major

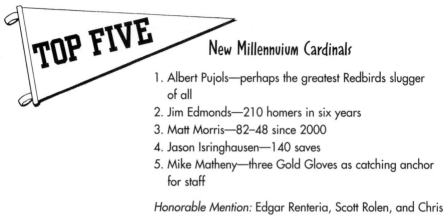

TOP FIVE

New Millennium Cardinals

1. Albert Pujols—perhaps the greatest Redbirds slugger of all
2. Jim Edmonds—210 homers in six years
3. Matt Morris—82–48 since 2000
4. Jason Isringhausen—140 saves
5. Mike Matheny—three Gold Gloves as catching anchor for staff

Honorable Mention: Edgar Renteria, Scott Rolen, and Chris Carpenter

threat in its half of the inning, loading the bases with one out. When Morgan Ensberg lifted a sacrifice fly, the Astros were up, 2–1. La Russa was not around by that time, having been ejected for complaining about home-plate umpire Phil Cuzzi's tight strike-zone calls on Marquis' pitches. Later Jim Edmonds was tossed by a seemingly overly sensitive Cuzzi when he questioned what appeared to be a dubious strike call. Despite the drama, the big news was that Houston took a 2–1 win and had the Cardinals' backs up against the wall.

In Game 5 the Cardinals took a 2–1 lead in the third off Andy Pettitte, and Chris Carpenter carried the one-run margin into the seventh. In the bottom of the seventh, the Astros struck with three huge runs on a three-run shot by clutch-hitting Lance Berkman. The Cardinals went quietly in the eighth, and the champagne was readied in the Houston locker room as the Redbirds came to bat in the ninth against their nemesis, Brad Lidge.

Lidge was dominating, striking out both John Rodriguez and John Mabry to open the inning. He then jumped ahead 1–2 on pesky David Eckstein, the Cardinals leadoff man. Eckstein managed to push a seemingly harmless single into left field to keep the game flickering. Jim Edmonds then battled Lidge for a walk. With one strike on him, the great Albert Pujols devoured a hanging slider, driving it 412 feet over the train tracks beyond left field, and the Cardinals were shockingly in the lead, 5–4.

The Astros had been one strike away from the World Series. In a seemingly stunned trance, the Astros went obediently in the ninth against Redbirds closer Jason Isringhausen, and the rejuvenated Cardinals were on their way back home, within a game of evening the series against the Astros.

The psychological wind was at the Cardinals' back as trusty left-hander Mark Mulder headed for the mound in front of 52,438 adoring St. Louis fans in the final series ever to be played at the then-current Busch Stadium. Garner countered with 20-game-winner Roy Oswalt, the Game 2 winner. The game was scoreless through the first two innings, and Redbirds fans settled in, expecting a nail-biter. In the top of the third, Mulder uncharacteristically threw a wild pitch that allowed Brad Ausmus in from third, and when Craig Biggio singled, Adam Everett came in with the second run. After five innings the 'Stros held a 3–1 lead, and the St. Louis crowd realized runs would be hard to muster off the scintillating Oswalt.

Houston added a run in each of the next two innings, and when Oswalt left after the seventh, his mates had handed him a 5–1 lead. After Chad Qualls and Dan Wheeler delivered scoreless efforts in the eighth and the ninth, the Houston Astros were the NLCS winners.

Looking Ahead

If you are a baseball fan, when you hear St. Louis, you think Cardinals. How could you not? The baseball Cardinals have not only survived long after the baseball Browns, the football Cardinals, and the basketball Hawks have left St. Louis, but they have also thrived. They have stamped the word *winner* on the very identity of the city.

This stamp was never more indelible than in the first six years of the new millennium. The Cardinals have won one pennant, four divisional series, and four Central Division titles. They have played 178 games over .500 in the past six seasons and averaged just short of 96 wins per season, totaling 575 over the span. That is the best record in the National League. Only Atlanta, with 571, is even close. Moreover, the Cardinals have never begun a decade with such sustained success. All that is missing is another World Series championship, which would be the organization's first since 1982.

TRIVIA

What milestone did Tony La Russa reach in 2005?

Answers to the trivia questions are on pages 161–162.

There is reason to look ahead with excitement.

The St. Louis Cardinals are truly a great organization, with an outstanding GM and a Hall of Fame manager with an excellent coaching staff. These pieces form the foundation for the building of great teams, teams that will play in front of more than 3 million Redbirds fans each season in a sparkling new ballpark.

It is great to be a Cardinals fan.

By the **NUMBERS** **1,795–1,427**—Record with which the Cardinals closed Busch Stadium.

ANSWERS TO
TRIVIA QUESTIONS

Page 4: Tony La Russa, Whitey Herzog, and Red Schoendienst have managed the Cardinals for part or all of at least 10 seasons.

Page 7: Fifty-two years later, in 1954, the St. Louis Browns became the Baltimore Orioles.

Page 9: Branch Rickey's nickname was "the Mahatma," in recognition of his baseball savvy and his aristocratic air and eloquent speech.

Page 15: Ronald Reagan played the role of Grover Cleveland Alexander in the Hollywood film *The Winning Team*. In that movie Alexander finished the game with a strikeout.

Page 19: Alexander pitched for the Cubs prior to going to St. Louis.

Page 22: Bill Veeck, owner of the Cleveland Indians, broke the color line in the American League when he brought up Larry Doby in 1947.

Page 27: Rogers Hornsby, with 164 home runs and 787 RBIs, and Jim Bottomley, with 146 home runs and 905 RBIs, dominated the Cardinals in home runs and RBIs in the twenties.

Page 30: Frisch was well known for dominating the Hall of Fame's Veteran Committee and helping a long list of sometimes undeserving former teammates get into the Hall.

Page 31: Branch Rickey is the only man to have been in the Cardinals dugout as manager longer than Frisch, from 1919 to 1925.

Page 35: Babe Didrikson Zaharias pitched an inning for the Cardinals in a 1934 exhibition game.

Page 37: Sandy Koufax, like Dean, had only 165 wins, 97 of which came in four seasons.

Page 42: Branch Rickey said Durocher had a special capacity for making a bad situation worse.

Page 44: Durocher is famous for saying, "Nice guys finish last."

Page 45: Leo Durocher, who was inducted into the Hall of Fame as a manager, never managed the Cardinals.

Page 48: In 1934 Tex Carleton was third in wins for the Cardinals, going 16–11, and Bill Walker went 12–4.

Page 49: Medwick was seriously beaned by former Cardinals teammate Bob Bowman six days after being traded to Brooklyn. Bowman was angry about being taunted in an elevator.

Page 51: Lon Warneke stayed in the game after his pitching career was over by becoming an umpire.

Page 56: Johnny Mize hit three home runs in a single game six times.

Page 59: The 1945 All-Star Game was cancelled because of wartime traveling restrictions.

Page 60: The war did not have an effect on major league attendance. Despite the watered-down rosters, major league attendance hit 10.28 million, breaking the 1940 record.

Page 64: In Cardinals history the 1942 team's 106–48 record ranks first.

Page 72: Vinegar Bend Mizell was second in wins in the fifties with 69; Harvey Haddix and Larry Jackson each had 53, although Jackson added 48 during the sixties.

Page 76: Ken Boyer was the 1964 MVP.

Page 80: Curt Flood led the Cardinals in hits during the sixties with 1,690.

Page 82: The following five pitchers had between 68 and 61 wins in the sixties: Ray Washburn (68), Ray Sadecki (68), Nelson Briles (63), Curt Simmons (62), and Ernie Broglio (61).

Page 85: During the sixties, Bill White was second to Ken Boyer with 128 home runs, and Curt Flood was second with 566 RBIs—White had 555.

Page 90: Only August A. Busch Jr. served as Cardinals president for longer than Sam Breadon, from 1953 to 1989.

Page 93: Hernandez shared the 1979 MVP with Willie Stargell.

Page 94: Ted Simmons led the Cardinals in home runs in the seventies with 151.

Page 98: Once he had Sutter, Herzog traded Rollie Fingers.

Page 103: The Cardinals bullpen was called Bullpen by Committee after Sutter left in 1985.

Page 113: Ray Lankford led the Cardinals in home runs during the nineties with 181. Mark McGwire was actually second for the decade, hitting 159 out of the park.

Page 119: No Cardinal but Stan Musial won the MVP award more than once.

Page 121: Three Cardinals pitchers have been named MVP: Dizzy Dean, Mort Cooper, and Bob Gibson.

Page 124: Alan is the name of Andy Benes' brother who also pitched for the Cardinals in 2000.

Page 127: Fernando Vina led the Cardinals in triples in 2001 with eight.

Page 132: Matt Morris was the only Cardinal to be named to both the 2001 and the 2002 All-Star teams.

Page 137: Scott Rolen led the Cardinals in RBIs in 2004, with 124.

Page 139: Houston was the only NL team against which the Cardinals had a losing regular-season record (8–10) in 2004.

Page 143: As a player, La Russa's primary defensive position was second base.

Page 154: Published in 2004, *Three Nights in August* focused on manager Tony La Russa.

Page 157: Lefty Ray King led the Cardinals pitching staff in appearances (77) in 2005.

Page 159: In 2005 Tony La Russa moved into third place among managers on the all-time win list, finishing the season with 2,214 victories.

St. Louis Cardinals All-Time Roster

Listed players have appeared in at least one game with the Cardinals. Players whose positions are indicated with a dash never played in the field and were used only as pinch-hitters or designated hitters.

A

Ody Abbott	Outfielder	1910
Ted Abernathy	Pitcher	1970
Juan Acevedo	Pitcher	1998–1999
Babe Adams	Pitcher	1906
Buster Adams	Outfielder	1939, 1943,
Jim Adams	Catcher	1890
Joe Adams	Pitcher	1902
Sparky Adams	Second Base	1930–1933
		1945–1946
Jim Adduci	Outfielder	1983
Henry Adkinson	Outfielder	1895
Tommie Agee	Outfielder	1973
Juan Agosto	Pitcher	1991–1992
Eddie Ainsmith	Catcher	1921–1923
Gibson Alba	Pitcher	1988
Cy Alberts	Pitcher	1910
Grover Alexander	Pitcher	1926–1929
Nin Alexander	Catcher	1884
Luis Alicea	Second Base	1988,
		1991–1994, 1996
Dick Allen	First Base	1970
Ethan Allen	Outfielder	1933
Neil Allen	Pitcher	1983–1985
Ron Allen	First Base	1972

Armando Almanza	Pitcher	2005
Matty Alou	Outfielder	1971–1973
Tom Alston	First Base	1954–1957
Walter Alston	First Base	1936
George Altman	Outfielder	1963
Luis Alvarado	Shortstop	1974, 1974, 1976
Brant Alyea	Outfielder	1972
Ruben Amaro	Shortstop	1958
Red Ames	Pitcher	1915–1919
Craig Anderson	Pitcher	1961
Dwain Anderson	Shortstop	1972–1973
Ferrell Anderson	Catcher	1953
George Anderson	Outfielder	1918
John Anderson	Pitcher	1962
Marlon Anderson	Second Base	2004
Mike Anderson	Outfielder	1976–1977
John Andrews	Pitcher	1973
Nate Andrews	Pitcher	1937, 1939
Joaquin Andujar	Pitcher	1981–1985
Pat Ankenman	Second Base	1936
Rick Ankiel	Pitcher	1999–2001, 2004
John Antonelli	Third Base	1944–1945
Harry Arndt	Second Base	1905–1907
Scott Arnold	Pitcher	1988
Rene Arocha	Pitcher	1993–1995
Luis Arroyo	Pitcher	1955
Rudy Arroyo	Pitcher	1971
Dennis Aust	Pitcher	1965–1966
Benny Ayala	Outfielder	1977
Manny Aybar	Pitcher	1997–1999

B

Les Backman	Pitcher	1909–1910
Bill Bailey	Pitcher	1921–1922
Cory Bailey	Pitcher	1995–1996
Doug Bair	Pitcher	1981–1983, 1985
Doug Baird	Third Base	1917–1919
Dave Bakenhaster	Pitcher	1964
Bill Baker	Catcher	1948–1949
Steve Baker	Pitcher	1983
O. F. Baldwin	Pitcher	1908
Ryan Balfe	—	2001–2002
Art Ball	Third Base	1894
Jimmy Bannon	Outfielder	1893
Jap Barbeau	Third Base	1909–1910
Brian Barber	Pitcher	1995–1996
George Barclay	Outfielder	1902–1904
Ray Bare	Pitcher	1972, 1974
Clyde Barfoot	Pitcher	1922–1923
Greg Bargar	Pitcher	1986
Sam Barkley	Second Base	1885
Mike Barlow	Pitcher	1975
Brian Barnes	Pitcher	1998–1999
Frank Barnes	Pitcher	1957–1958, 1960
Skeeter Barnes	Third Base	1987
Frank Barrett	Pitcher	1939
Red Barrett	Pitcher	1945–1946
Shad Barry	Outfielder	1906–1908
Dave Bartosch	Outfielder	1945
Rich Batchelor	Pitcher	1993, 1996–1997
Frank Bates	Pitcher	1899
Allen Battle	Outfielder	1995
Ed Bauta	Pitcher	1960–1963
Jose Bautista	Pitcher	1997
Moose Baxter	First Base	1907
Johnny Beall	Outfielder	1918
Ralph Beard	Pitcher	1954
Jim Beauchamp	First Base	1963, 1970–1971
Johnny Beazley	Pitcher	1941–1942, 1946
Zinn Beck	Third Base	1913–1916
Jake Beckley	First Base	1904–1907
Bill Beckmann	Pitcher	1942
Fred Beebe	Pitcher	1906–1909

Clarence Beers	Pitcher	1948
David Bell	Third Base	1995–1998
Hi Bell	Pitcher	1924, 1926, 1929–1930
Les Bell	Third Base	1923–1927
Jack Bellman	Catcher	1889
Rigo Beltran	Pitcher	1997
Alan Benes	Pitcher	1995–1997, 1999–2001
Andy Benes	Pitcher	1996–1997, 2000–2002
Joe Benes	Shortstop	1931
Gary Bennett	Catcher	2005 (Present)
Pug Bennett	Second Base	1906–1907
Vern Benson	Third Base	1951–1953
Sid Benton	Pitcher	1922
Jeff Berblinger	Second Base	1997
Augie Bergamo	Outfielder	1944–1945
Brandon Berger	Outfielder	2005
Jack Berly	Pitcher	1924
Joe Bernard	Pitcher	1909
Frank Bertaina	Pitcher	1970
Harry Berte	Second Base	1903
Bob Bescher	Outfielder	1915–1917
Frank Betcher	Shortstop	1910
Harry Betts	Pitcher	1903
Bruno Betzel	Second Base	1914–1918
Jim Bibby	Pitcher	1972–1973
Ed Biecher	Outfielder	1897
Lou Bierbauer	Second Base	1897–1898
Steve Bieser	Outfielder	2000
Larry Bigbie	Outfielder	2005 (Present)
Steve Bilko	First Base	1949–1954
Dick Billings	Catcher	1974–1975
Frank Bird	Catcher	1892
Ray Blades	Outfielder	1922–1928, 1930–1932
Harry Blake	Outfielder	1899
Sheriff Blake	Pitcher	1937
Coonie Blank	Catcher	1909
Don Blasingame	Second Base	1955–1959
Johnny Blatnik	Outfielder	1950

Name	Position	Years
Buddy Blattner	Second Base	1942
Bob Blaylock	Pitcher	1956, 1959
Gary Blaylock	Pitcher	1959
Jack Bliss	Catcher	1908–1912
Bud Bloomfield	Second Base	1963
Charlie Boardman	Pitcher	1915
Joe Boever	Pitcher	1985–1986
Sam Bohne	Second Base	1916
Dick Bokelmann	Pitcher	1951–1953
Bill Bolden	Pitcher	1919
Don Bollweg	First Base	1950–1951
Bobby Bonds	Outfielder	1980
Bobby Bonilla	Third Base	2001
Frank Bonner	Second Base	1895
Rod Booker	Shortstop	1987–1989
Pedro Borbon	Pitcher	1980
Pedro Borbon	Pitcher	2003
Frenchy Bordagaray	Outfielder	1937–1938
Pat Borders	Catcher	1996
Rick Bosetti	Outfielder	1977
Ricky Bottalico	Pitcher	1999
Kent Bottenfield	Pitcher	1998–1999
Jim Bottomley	First Base	1922–1932
Bob Bowman	Pitcher	1939–1940
Cloyd Boyer	Pitcher	1949–1952
Ken Boyer	Third Base	1955–1965
Jack Boyle	Catcher	1887–1889, 1891
Buddy Bradford	Outfielder	1975
Terry Bradshaw	Outfielder	1995–1996
Darren Bragg	Outfielder	1999
Dave Brain	Third Base	1903–1905
Harvey Branch	Pitcher	1962
Jackie Brandt	Outfielder	1956
Jeff Brantley	Pitcher	1998
Roy Brashear	First Base	1902
Joe Bratcher	Outfielder	1924
Steve Braun	Outfielder	1981–1985
Al Brazle	Pitcher	1943, 1946–1954
Harry Brecheen	Pitcher	1940, 1943–1952
Ted Breitenstein	Pitcher	1891–1896, 1901
Herb Bremer	Catcher	1937–1939
Roger Bresnahan	Catcher	1909–1912
Rube Bressler	Outfielder	1932
Eddie Bressoud	Shortstop	1967
Rod Brewer	First Base	1990–1993
Marshall Bridges	Pitcher	1959–1960
Rocky Bridges	Shortstop	1960
Grant Briggs	Catcher	1892
Nelson Briles	Pitcher	1965–1970
Ed Brinkman	Shortstop	1975
John Brock	Catcher	1917–1918
Lou Brock	Outfielder	1964–1979
Steve Brodie	Outfielder	1892–1893
Ernie Broglio	Pitcher	1959–1964
Herman Bronkie	Third Base	1918
Jim Brosnan	Pitcher	1958–1959
Tony Brottem	Catcher	1916, 1918
Cal Broughton	Catcher	1885
Buster Brown	Pitcher	1905–1907
Ed Brown	Third Base	1882
Jim Brown	Outfielder	1915
Jimmy Brown	Second Base	1937–1943
Mordecai Brown	Pitcher	1903
Tom Brown	Outfielder	1895
Willard Brown	First Base	1894
Byron Browne	Outfielder	1969
Cal Browning	Pitcher	1960
Pete Browning	Outfielder	1894
Glenn Brummer	Catcher	1981–1984
Tom Brunansky	Outfielder	1988–1990
George Brunet	Pitcher	1971
Justin Brunette	Pitcher	2000
Tom Bruno	Pitcher	1978–1979
Ron Bryant	Pitcher	1975
Johnny Bucha	Catcher	1948, 1950
Jerry Buchek	Second Base	1961, 1963–1966
Jim Bucher	Third Base	1938
Gary Buckels	Pitcher	1994
Dick Buckley	Catcher	1892–1894
Fritz Buelow	Catcher	1899–1900
Nelson Burbrink	Catcher	1955
Al Burch	Outfielder	1906–1907
Bob Burda	First Base	1962, 1971

Lew Burdette	Pitcher	1963–1964
Tom Burgess	First Base	1954
Sandy Burk	Pitcher	1912–1913
Jimmy Burke	Third Base	1899, 1903–1905
Joe Burke	Third Base	1890
Leo Burke	Outfielder	1963
Jesse Burkett	Outfielder	1899–1901
Ken Burkhart	Pitcher	1945–1948
Jack Burnett	Outfielder	1907
Ed Burns	Catcher	1912
Farmer Burns	Pitcher	1901
Todd Burns	Pitcher	1993
Harry Burrell	Pitcher	1891
Ray Burris	Pitcher	1986
Ellis Burton	Outfielder	1958, 1960
Mike Busby	Pitcher	1996–1999
Guy Bush	Pitcher	1938
Doc Bushong	Catcher	1885–1887
Ray Busse	Shortstop	1973
Art Butler	Shortstop	1914–1916
John Butler	Catcher	1904
Johnny Butler	Shortstop	1929
Bud Byerly	Pitcher	1943–1945
Bill Byers	Catcher	1904
Bobby Byrne	Third Base	1907–1909

C

Al Cabrera	Shortstop	1913
Miguel Cairo	Second Base	2001–2003
Kiko Calero	Pitcher	2003–2004
Jack Calhoun	Third Base	1902
Carmen Cali	Pitcher	2004–2005 (Present)
John Callahan	Pitcher	1898
Wesley Callahan	Shortstop	1913
Ernie Camacho	Pitcher	1990
Harry Camnitz	Pitcher	1911
Lew Camp	Third Base	1892
Count Campau	Outfielder	1890
Bill Campbell	Pitcher	1985
Billy Campbell	Pitcher	1905
Dave Campbell	Second Base	1973

Jim Campbell	—	1970
Sal Campisi	Pitcher	1969–1970
Chris Cannizzaro	Catcher	1960–1961
Ozzie Canseco	Outfielder	1992–1993
Doug Capilla	Pitcher	1976–1977
Chance Caple	Pitcher	2003
Ramon Caraballo	Second Base	1995
Bernie Carbo	Outfielder	1972–1973, 1979–1980
Jose Cardenal	Outfielder	1970–1971
Tex Carleton	Pitcher	1932–1934
Steve Carlton	Pitcher	1965–1971
Duke Carmel	Outfielder	1959–1960, 1963
Chris Carpenter	Pitcher	2004–2005 (Present)
Cris Carpenter	Pitcher	1988–1992
Hick Carpenter	Third Base	1892
Chuck Carr	Outfielder	1992
Clay Carroll	Pitcher	1977
Cliff Carroll	Outfielder	1892
Kid Carsey	Pitcher	1897–1898
Ed Cartwright	First Base	1890
Bob Caruthers	Outfielder	1884–1887, 1892
Pete Castiglione	Third Base	1953–1954
Alberto Castillo	Catcher	1999
Danny Cater	First Base	1975
Ted Cather	Outfielder	1912–1914
Cesar Cedeno	Outfielder	1985
Roger Cedeno	Left Field	2004–2005
Orlando Cepeda	First Base	1966–1968
Elton Chamberlain	Pitcher	1888–1890
Bill Chambers	Pitcher	1910
Cliff Chambers	Pitcher	1951–1953
Johnnie Chambers	Pitcher	1937
Charlie Chant	Outfielder	1976
Carlos Chantres	Pitcher	2003
Chappy Charles	Second Base	1908–1909
Tom Cheney	Pitcher	1957, 1959
Cupid Childs	Second Base	1899
Pete Childs	Second Base	1901
Nelson Chittum	Pitcher	1958
Bob Chlupsa	Pitcher	1970–1971

Name	Position	Years
Jason Christiansen	Pitcher	2000–2001
Larry Ciaffone	Outfielder	1951
Al Cicotte	Pitcher	1961
Gino Cimoli	Outfielder	1959
Frank Cimorelli	Pitcher	1994
Ralph Citarella	Pitcher	1983–1984
Stubby Clapp	Second Base	2001
Doug Clarey	Second Base	1976
Danny Clark	Third Base	1927
Jack Clark	Outfielder	1985–1987
Jim Clark	Outfielder	1911–1912
Mark Clark	Pitcher	1991–1992
Mike Clark	Pitcher	1952–1953
Phil Clark	Pitcher	1958–1959
Will Clark	First Base	2000
Josh Clarke	Outfielder	1905
Stan Clarke	Pitcher	1990
Dad Clarkson	Pitcher	1893–1895
Royce Clayton	Shortstop	1996–1998
Doug Clemens	Outfielder	1960–1964
Jack Clements	Catcher	1898
Lance Clemons	Pitcher	1972
Verne Clemons	Catcher	1919–1924
Donn Clendenon	First Base	1972
Reggie Cleveland	Pitcher	1969–1973
Tony Cloninger	Pitcher	1972
Ed Clough	Outfielder	1924–1926
Dick Cole	Shortstop	1951
Percy Coleman	Pitcher	1897
Vince Coleman	Outfielder	1985–1990
Walter Coleman	Pitcher	1895
Darnell Coles	Third Base	1995
Dave Collins	Outfielder	1990
Phil Collins	Pitcher	1935
Ripper Collins	First Base	1931–1936
(Unknown) Collins	Outfielder	1892
Jackie Collum	Pitcher	1951–1953, 1956
Bob Coluccio	Outfielder	1978
Charlie Comiskey	First Base	1882–1889, 1891
Joe Connor	Catcher	1895
Roger Connor	First Base	1894–1897
Tim Conroy	Pitcher	1986–1987
Ed Conwell	Third Base	1911
Paul Cook	Catcher	1891
Mike Coolbaugh	Third Base	2002
Scott Coolbaugh	Third Base	1994
Duff Cooley	Outfielder	1893–1896
Jimmy Cooney	Shortstop	1924–1925
Mort Cooper	Pitcher	1938–1945
Scott Cooper	Third Base	1995
Walker Cooper	Catcher	1940–1945, 1956–1957
Mays Copeland	Pitcher	1935
Joe Corbett	Pitcher	1904
Brent Cordell	Catcher	2005
Roy Corhan	Shortstop	1916
Rheal Cormier	Pitcher	1991–1994
Pat Corrales	Catcher	1966
Frank Corridon	Pitcher	1910
Jim Cosman	Pitcher	1966–1967
John Costello	Pitcher	1988–1990
Chip Coulter	Second Base	1969
Jack Coveney	Catcher	1903
Bill Cox	Pitcher	1936
Danny Cox	Pitcher	1983–1988
Estel Crabtree	Outfielder	1933, 1941–1942
Roger Craig	Pitcher	1964
Doc Crandall	Pitcher	1913
Forrest Crawford	Shortstop	1906–1907
Glenn Crawford	Outfielder	1945
Pat Crawford	Second Base	1933–1934
Willie Crawford	Outfielder	1976
Doug Creek	Pitcher	1995
Jack Creel	Pitcher	1945
Gus Creely	Shortstop	1890
Bernie Creger	Shortstop	1947
Creepy Crespi	Second Base	1938–1942
Brad Cresse	Catcher	2005
Lou Criger	Catcher	1899–1900
Jack Crimian	Pitcher	1951–1952
Morrie Critchley	Pitcher	1882
Tripp Cromer	Shortstop	1993–1995
Jack Crooks	Second Base	1892–1893, 1898

Ed Crosby	Shortstop	1970, 1972–1973	Eric Davis	Outfielder	1999–2000
			Jim Davis	Pitcher	1957
Jeff Cross	Shortstop	1942, 1946–1948	Jumbo Davis	Third Base	1889–1890
Lave Cross	Third Base	1898–1900	Kiddo Davis	Outfielder	1934
Monte Cross	Shortstop	1896–1897	Ron Davis	Outfielder	1968
Joe Crotty	Catcher	1882	Spud Davis	Catcher	1928, 1934–1936
Bill Crouch	Pitcher	1941, 1941, 1945	Willie Davis	Outfielder	1975
Rick Croushore	Pitcher	1998–1999	Bill Dawley	Pitcher	1987
George Crowe	First Base	1959–1961	Boots Day	Outfielder	1969
Mike Crudale	Pitcher	2002–2003	Pea Ridge Day	Pitcher	1924–1925
Walton Cruise	Outfielder	1914, 1916–1919	Ken Dayley	Pitcher	1984–1990
Gene Crumling	Catcher	1945	Carlos De La Cruz	Center Field	2005
Deivi Cruz	Shortstop	2005 (Present)	Mike DeJean	Pitcher	2003
Hector Cruz	Outfielder	1973, 1975–1977	Delino DeShields	Second Base	1997–1998
Ivan Cruz	First Base	2002	Cot Deal	Pitcher	1950, 1954
Jose Cruz	Outfielder	1970–1974	Dizzy Dean	Pitcher	1930, 1932–1937
Tommy Cruz	Outfielder	1973	Paul Dean	Pitcher	1934–1939
Mike Cuellar	Pitcher	1964	Pat Deasley	Catcher	1883–1884
George Culver	Pitcher	1970	Doug Decinces	Third Base	1987
John Cumberland	Pitcher	1972	Frank Decker	Catcher	1882
Jeremy Cummings	Pitcher	2005	George Decker	Outfielder	1898
Joe Cunningham	First Base	1954, 1956–1961	Tony Defate	Third Base	1917
Ray Cunningham	Third Base	1931–1932	Rube Degroff	Outfielder	1905–1906
Nig Cuppy	Pitcher	1899	Ivan Dejesus	Shortstop	1985
Clarence Currie	Pitcher	1902–1903	Joe Delahanty	Outfielder	1907–1909
Murphy Currie	Pitcher	1916	Bill Delancey	Catcher	1932, 1934, 1935, 1940
John Curtis	Pitcher	1974–1976			
Ned Cuthbert	Outfielder	1882–1883	Art Delaney	Pitcher	1924
			Jose Deleon	Pitcher	1988–1992
D			Luis Deleon	Pitcher	1981
John D'Acquisto	Pitcher	1977	Wilson Delgado	Second Base	2002–2003
Gene Dale	Pitcher	1911–1912	Bobby Delgreco	Outfielder	1956
Jack Damaska	Second Base	1963	Eddie Delker	Second Base	1929, 1931–1932
Pete Daniels	Pitcher	1898	Wheezer Dell	Pitcher	1912
Rolla Daringer	Shortstop	1914–1915	Rich Delucia	Pitcher	1995
Alvin Dark	Shortstop	1956–1958	Frank Demaree	Outfielder	1943
Dell Darling	Catcher	1891	Lee Demontreville	Shortstop	1903
Vic Davalillo	Outfielder	1969–1970	Don Dennis	Pitcher	1965–1966
Jerry Davanon	Shortstop	1969–1970, 1974, 1977	John Denny	Pitcher	1974–1979
			Paul Derringer	Pitcher	1931–1933
Curt Davis	Pitcher	1938–1940	Russ Derry	Outfielder	1949
Daisy Davis	Pitcher	1884	Joe Desa	First Base	1980

Jim Devlin	Pitcher	1888–1889		Matt Duff	Pitcher	2002
Mike DiFelice	Catcher	1996–1997, 2002		Charlie Duffee	Outfielder	1889–1890
Einar Diaz	Catcher	2005 (Present)		Bob Duliba	Pitcher	1959–1960, 1962
Leo Dickerman	Pitcher	1924–1925		Chris Duncan	First Base	2005 (Present)
Murry Dickson	Pitcher	1939–1940, 1942,		Taylor Duncan	Third Base	1977
		1946–1948,		Wiley Dunham	Pitcher	1902
		1956–1957		Grant Dunlap	Outfielder	1953
Chuck Diering	Outfielder	1947–1951		Jack Dunleavy	Outfielder	1903–1905
Larry Dierker	Pitcher	1977		Shawon Dunston	Shortstop	1999–2000
Pat Dillard	Outfielder	1900		Don Durham	Pitcher	1972
Pickles Dillhoefer	Catcher	1919–1921		Leon Durham	First Base	1980, 1980, 1989
Mike Dimmel	Outfielder	1979		Joe Durham	Outfielder	1959
Frank Dipino	Pitcher	1989–1990, 1992		Leo Durocher	Shortstop	1933–1937
Dutch Distel	Second Base	1918		Jesse Duryea	Pitcher	1891
Steve Dixon	Pitcher	1993–1994		Erv Dusak	Outfielder	1941–1942,
Bill Doak	Pitcher	1913–1924, 1929				1946–1951
George Dockins	Pitcher	1945		Frank Dwyer	Pitcher	1892
Cozy Dolan	Outfielder	1914–1915		Jim Dwyer	Outfielder	1973–1975,
John Dolan	Pitcher	1893				1977–1978
Tom Dolan	Catcher	1883–1884, 1888		Eddie Dyer	Pitcher	1922–1927
Red Donahue	Pitcher	1895–1897				
She Donahue	Shortstop	1904		**E**		
Mike Donlin	Outfielder	1899–1900		Bill Eagan	Second Base	1891
Blix Donnelly	Pitcher	1944–1946		Billy Earle	Catcher	1890
Jim Donnelly	Third Base	1890, 1890, 1898		Bill Earley	Pitcher	1986
Patsy Donovan	Outfielder	1900–1903		George Earnshaw	Pitcher	1936
Bert Dorr	Pitcher	1882		Jack Easton	Pitcher	1891–1892
Jim Dougherty	Pitcher	2000		Rawly Eastwick	Pitcher	1977
Klondike Douglass	First Base	1896–1897		Johnny Echols	—	1939
Taylor Douthit	Outfielder	1923–1931		Dennis Eckersley	Pitcher	1996–1997
Tommy Dowd	Outfielder	1893–1898		Al Eckert	Pitcher	1935
Dave Dowling	Pitcher	1964		David Eckstein	Shortstop	2005
Carl Doyle	Pitcher	1940				(Present)
Jeff Doyle	Second Base	1983		Joe Edelen	Pitcher	1981
John Doyle	Pitcher	1882		Jim Edmonds	Outfielder	2000–2005
Moe Drabowsky	Pitcher	1971–1972				(Present)
Lee Dressen	First Base	1914		Johnny Edwards	Catcher	1968
Rob Dressler	Pitcher	1978		Wish Egan	Pitcher	1905–1906
J. D. Drew	Outfielder	1998–2003		Red Ehret	Pitcher	1895
Dan Driessen	First Base	1987		Cal Eldred	Pitcher	2003–2005
Mike Drissel	Catcher	1885				(Present)
Carl Druhot	Pitcher	1906–1907		Harry Elliott	Outfielder	1953, 1955

Jim Ellis	Pitcher	1969
Rube Ellis	Outfielder	1909–1912
Bones Ely	Shortstop	1893–1895
Bill Endicott	Outfielder	1946
Del Ennis	Outfielder	1957–1958
Charlie Enwright	Shortstop	1909
Hal Epps	Outfielder	1938, 1940
Eddie Erautt	Pitcher	1953
Duke Esper	Pitcher	1897–1898
Brian Esposito	Catcher	2005
Chuck Essegian	Outfielder	1959
Roy Evans	Pitcher	1897
Steve Evans	Outfielder	1909–1913
Bryan Eversgerd	Pitcher	1994, 1998
Bob Ewing	Pitcher	1912
John Ewing	Pitcher	1883
Reuben Ewing	Shortstop	1921

F

Fred Fagin	Catcher	1895
Ron Fairly	First Base	1975–1976
Pete Falcone	Pitcher	1976–1978
George Fallon	Second Base	1943–1945
Harry Fanok	Pitcher	1963–1964
Doc Farrell	Shortstop	1930
John Farrell	Second Base	1902–1905
Jeff Fassero	Pitcher	2002–2003
Jack Faszholz	Pitcher	1953
Bobby Fenwick	Second Base	1973
Joe Ferguson	Catcher	1976
Don Ferrarese	Pitcher	1962
Neil Fiala	—	1981
Bien Figueroa	Shortstop	1992
Bob File	Pitcher	2005
Chuck Finley	Pitcher	2002
Mike Fiore	First Base	1972
Sam Fishburn	First Base	1919
Bob Fisher	Shortstop	1918–1919
Chauncey Fisher	Pitcher	1901
Eddie Fisher	Pitcher	1973
Showboat Fisher	Outfielder	1930
Mike Fitzgerald	First Base	1988

Max Flack	Outfielder	1922–1925
Tom Flanigan	Pitcher	1958
Curt Flood	Outfielder	1958–1969
Tim Flood	Second Base	1899
Randy Flores	Pitcher	2004–2005 (Present)
Ben Flowers	Pitcher	1955–1956
Jake Flowers	Second Base	1923, 1926, 1931–1932
Rich Folkers	Pitcher	1972–1974
Curt Ford	Outfielder	1985–1988
Hod Ford	Shortstop	1932
Bob Forsch	Pitcher	1974–1988
Tony Fossas	Pitcher	1995–1997
Alan Foster	Pitcher	1973–1974
Jack Fournier	First Base	1920–1922
Dave Foutz	First Base	1884–1887
Jesse Fowler	Pitcher	1924
Earl Francis	Pitcher	1965
Tito Francona	Outfielder	1965–1966
Charlie Frank	Outfielder	1893–1894
Fred Frankhouse	Pitcher	1927–1930
Micah Franklin	Outfielder	1997
Herman Franks	Catcher	1939
John Frascatore	Pitcher	1994–1995, 1997–1998
Willie Fraser	Pitcher	1991
George Frazier	Pitcher	1978–1980
Joe Frazier	Outfielder	1954–1956
Roger Freed	Outfielder	1977–1979
Julie Freeman	Pitcher	1888
Gene Freese	Third Base	1958
Howard Freigau	Third Base	1922–1925
Benny Frey	Pitcher	1932
Frankie Frisch	Second Base	1927–1937
Danny Frisella	Pitcher	1976
Art Fromme	Pitcher	1906–1908
John Fulgham	Pitcher	1979–1980
Harry Fuller	Third Base	1891
Shorty Fuller	Shortstop	1889–1891
Chick Fullis	Outfielder	1934, 1936
Chick Fulmer	Shortstop	1884

Eddie Fusselback	Catcher	1882	Hal Gilson	Pitcher	1968
Les Fusselman	Catcher	1952–1953	Joe Girardi	Catcher	2003
			Chris Gissell	Pitcher	2005
G			Dave Giusti	Pitcher	1969
Gary Gaetti	Third Base	1996–1998	Jack Glasscock	Shortstop	1892–1893
Phil Gagliano	Second Base	1963–1970	Tommy Glaviano	Third Base	1949–1952
Del Gainer	First Base	1922	Bill Gleason	Shortstop	1882–1887
Fred Gaiser	Pitcher	1908	Jack Gleason	Third Base	1882–1883
Andres Galarraga	First Base	1992	Kid Gleason	Second Base	1892–1894
John Gall	Left Field	2005 (Present)	Bob Glenn	Pitcher	1920
Mike Gallego	Second Base	1996–1997	Harry Glenn	Catcher	1915
Jim Galloway	Second Base	1912	John Glenn	Outfielder	1960
Jim Galvin	Pitcher	1892	Danny Godby	Outfielder	1974
Joe Gannon	Pitcher	1898	Roy Golden	Pitcher	1910–1911
Ron Gant	Outfielder	1996–1998	Walt Goldsby	Outfielder	1884
Joe Garagiola	Catcher	1946–1951	Hal Goldsmith	Pitcher	1929
Danny Gardella	Outfielder	1950	Mike Gonzalez	Catcher	1915–1918,
Glenn Gardner	Pitcher	1945			1924, 1931–1932
Art Garibaldi	Third Base	1936	Julio Gonzalez	Second Base	1981–1982
Mike Garman	Pitcher	1974–1975	Bill Goodenough	Outfielder	1893
Debs Garms	Outfielder	1943–1945	Mike Goodfellow	Outfielder	1887
Wayne Garrett	Third Base	1978	Marv Goodwin	Pitcher	1917, 1919–1922
Matt Garrick	—	1999–2002	George Gore	Outfielder	1892
Rich Gedman	Catcher	1991–1992	Reid Gorecki	Center Field	2004–2005
Charlie Gelbert	Shortstop	1929–1932,			(Present)
		1935–1936	Jack Gorman	First Base	1883
Frank Genins	Outfielder	1892	Herb Gorman	—	1952
Joe Gerhardt	Second Base	1890	Hank Gornicki	Pitcher	1941
Al Gettel	Pitcher	1955	Julio Gotay	Shortstop	1960–1962
Tom Gettinger	Outfielder	1889–1890	Al Grabowski	Pitcher	1929–1930
Charlie Getzien	Pitcher	1892	Mike Grady	Catcher	1897, 1904–1906
Rube Geyer	Pitcher	1910–1913	Alex Grammas	Shortstop	1954–1956,
Ray Giannelli	Third Base	1995			1959–1962
Bob Gibson	Pitcher	1959–1975	Wayne Granger	Pitcher	1968, 1973
Billy Gilbert	Second Base	1908–1909	Mudcat Grant	Pitcher	1969
Shawn Gilbert	Outfielder	1998	Mark Grater	Pitcher	1991
George Gilham	Catcher	1920–1921	Dick Gray	Third Base	1959–1960
Frank Gilhooley	Outfielder	1911–1912	Bill Greason	Pitcher	1954
Bernard Gilkey	Outfielder	1990–1995	David Green	Outfielder	1981–1984,
Jim Gill	Second Base	1889			1987
Carden Gillenwater	Outfielder	1940	Gene Green	Outfielder	1957–1959
George Gillpatrick	Pitcher	1898	Scarborough Green	Outfielder	1997

Bill Greif	Pitcher	1976	Russ Hall	Shortstop	1898
Tim Griesenbeck	Catcher	1920	Bill Hallahan	Pitcher	1925–1926,
Tom Grieve	Outfielder	1979			1929–1936
Sandy Griffin	Outfielder	1893	Bill Hallman	Second Base	1897
Clark Griffith	Pitcher	1891	Dave Hamilton	Pitcher	1978
Bob Grim	Pitcher	1960	Fred Haney	Third Base	1929
Burleigh Grimes	Pitcher	1930–1931,	Larry Haney	Catcher	1973
		1933–1934	Ed Harding	Catcher	1886
John Grimes	Pitcher	1897	Danny Haren	Pitcher	2003–2004
Charlie Grimm	First Base	1918	Dick Harley	Outfielder	1897–1898
Dan Griner	Pitcher	1912–1916	Bob Harmon	Pitcher	1909–1913
Marv Grissom	Pitcher	1959	Chuck Harmon	Third Base	1956–1957
Dick Groat	Shortstop	1963–1965	Brian Harper	Catcher	1985
Johnny Grodzicki	Pitcher	1941, 1946–1947	George Harper	Outfielder	1928
Mark Grudzielanek	Second Base	2005 (Present)	Jack Harper	Pitcher	1900–1901
Joe Grzenda	Pitcher	1972	Ray Harrell	Pitcher	1935, 1937–1938
Mario Guerrero	Shortstop	1975	Vic Harris	Second Base	1976
Pedro Guerrero	First Base	1988–1992	Bill Hart	Pitcher	1896–1897
Wilton Guerrero	Second Base	2005	Billy Hart	Pitcher	1890
Lee Guetterman	Pitcher	1993	Bo Hart	Second Base	2003–2004
Mike Gulan	Third Base	1997			(Present)
Harry Gumbert	Pitcher	1941–1944	Chuck Hartenstein	Pitcher	1970
Joe Gunson	Catcher	1893	Fred Hartman	Third Base	1897, 1902
Don Gutteridge	Second Base	1936–1940	Pat Hartnett	First Base	1890
Santiago Guzman	Pitcher	1969–1972	Andy Hassler	Pitcher	1984–1985
			Grady Hatton	Third Base	1956
H			Arnold Hauser	Shortstop	1910–1913
Bob Habenicht	Pitcher	1951	Bill Hawke	Pitcher	1892–1893
John Habyan	Pitcher	1994–1995	Pink Hawley	Pitcher	1892–1894
Jim Hackett	First Base	1902–1903	Doc Hazleton	First Base	1902
Luther Hackman	Pitcher	2000–2002	Francis Healy	Catcher	1934
Harvey Haddix	Pitcher	1952–1956	Bunny Hearn	Pitcher	1910–1911
Chick Hafey	Outfielder	1924–1931	Jim Hearn	Pitcher	1947–1950
Casey Hageman	Pitcher	1914	Mike Heath	Catcher	1986
Kevin Hagen	Pitcher	1983–1984	Cliff Heathcote	Outfielder	1918–1922
Joe Hague	First Base	1968–1972	Jack Heidemann	Shortstop	1974
Don Hahn	Outfielder	1975	Emmet Heidrick	Outfielder	1899–1901
Fred Hahn	Pitcher	1952	Don Heinkel	Pitcher	1989
Hal Haid	Pitcher	1928–1930	Tom Heintzelman	Second Base	1973–1974
Ed Haigh	Outfielder	1892	Bob Heise	Shortstop	1974
Jesse Haines	Pitcher	1920–1937	Clarence Heise	Pitcher	1934
Charley Hall	Pitcher	1916	Rick Heiserman	Pitcher	1999

Scott Hemond	Catcher	1995	Aaron Holbert	Second Base	1996
Charlie Hemphill	Outfielder	1899	Mul Holland	Pitcher	1929
Solly Hemus	Shortstop	1949–1956, 1959	Ed Holly	Shortstop	1906–1907
George Hendrick	Outfielder	1978–1984	Wattie Holm	Outfielder	1924–1929, 1932
Harvey Hendrick	First Base	1932	Darren Holmes	Pitcher	2000
Tom Henke	Pitcher	1995	Ducky Holmes	Catcher	1906
Roy Henshaw	Pitcher	1938	Ducky Holmes	Outfielder	1898
Pat Hentgen	Pitcher	2000	Rick Honeycutt	Pitcher	1996–1997
Dustin Hermanson	Pitcher	2001, 2003	Don Hood	Pitcher	1980
Carlos Hernandez	Catcher	2000	Buck Hopkins	Outfielder	1907
Keith Hernandez	First Base	1974–1983	Johnny Hopp	Outfielder	1939–1945
Michael Hernandez	Catcher	2005 (Present)	Bill Hopper	Pitcher	1913–1914
Larry Herndon	Outfielder	1974	Bob Horner	Third Base	1988
Ed Herr	Shortstop	1888, 1890	Rogers Hornsby	Second Base	1915–1926, 1933
Tom Herr	Second Base	1979–1988	Oscar Horstmann	Pitcher	1917–1919
Neal Hertweck	First Base	1952	Ricky Horton	Pitcher	1984–1987,
Ed Heusser	Pitcher	1935–1936			1989–1990
Mike Heydon	Catcher	1901	Paul Householder	Outfielder	1984
Jim Hickman	Outfielder	1974	John Houseman	Second Base	1897
Jim Hicks	Outfielder	1969	David Howard	Shortstop	1998–1999
Irv Higginbotham	Pitcher	1906, 1908–1909	Doug Howard	First Base	1975
Bill Higgins	Second Base	1890	Earl Howard	Pitcher	1918
Dennis Higgins	Pitcher	1971–1972	Thomas Howard	Outfielder	1999–2000
Eddie Higgins	Pitcher	1909–1910	Art Howe	Third Base	1984–1985
Andy High	Third Base	1928–1931	Roland Howell	Pitcher	1912
Palmer Hildebrand	Catcher	1913	Bill Howerton	Outfielder	1949–1951
Tom Hilgendorf	Pitcher	1969–1970	Dummy Hoy	Outfielder	1891
Carmen Hill	Pitcher	1929–1930	Al Hrabosky	Pitcher	1970–1977
Hugh Hill	Outfielder	1904	John Hudek	Pitcher	2000
Ken Hill	Pitcher	1988–1991, 1995	Jimmy Hudgens	First Base	1923
Marc Hill	Catcher	1973–1974	Rex Hudler	Second Base	1990–1992
Howard Hilton	Pitcher	1990	Charlie Hudson	Pitcher	1972
Jack Himes	Outfielder	1905–1906	Nat Hudson	Pitcher	1886–1889
Sterling Hitchcock	Pitcher	2003	Frank Huelsman	Outfielder	1897
Bruce Hitt	Pitcher	1917	Miller Huggins	Second Base	1910–1916
Glen Hobbie	Pitcher	1964	Dick Hughes	Pitcher	1966–1968
Ed Hock	Outfielder	1920	Terry Hughes	Third Base	1973
Charlie Hodnett	Pitcher	1883	Tom Hughes	Pitcher	1959
Art Hoelskoetter	Second Base	1905–1908	Jim Hughey	Pitcher	1898, 1900
Joe Hoerner	Pitcher	1966–1969	Tim Hulett	Third Base	1995
Eddie Hogan	Outfielder	1882	David Hulse	Outfielder	1998–1999
Marty Hogan	Outfielder	1894–1895	Rudy Hulswitt	Shortstop	1909–1910

Bill Keister	Shortstop	1900
John Kelleher	Third Base	1912
Mick Kelleher	Shortstop	1972–1973, 1975
Alex Kellner	Pitcher	1959
Win Kellum	Pitcher	1905
Billy Kelly	Catcher	1910
John Kelly	Outfielder	1907
Pat Kelly	Second Base	1998
Rudy Kemmler	Catcher	1886
Adam Kennedy	Second Base	1999
Jim Kennedy	Shortstop	1970
Terry Kennedy	Catcher	1978–1980
Matt Keough	Pitcher	1985
Kurt Kepshire	Pitcher	1984–1986
John Kerins	First Base	1890
George Kernek	First Base	1965–1966
Don Kessinger	Shortstop	1976–1977
Darryl Kile	Pitcher	2000–2002
Paul Kilgus	Pitcher	1993
Newt Kimball	Pitcher	1940
Hal Kime	Pitcher	1920
Wally Kimmick	Shortstop	1919
Ellis Kinder	Pitcher	1956
Chick King	Outfielder	1959
Curtis King	Pitcher	1997–1999
Jim King	Outfielder	1957
Lynn King	Outfielder	1935–1936, 1939
Ray King	Pitcher	2004–2005 (Present)
Silver King	Pitcher	1887–1889
Walt Kinlock	Third Base	1895
Tom Kinslow	Catcher	1898
Matt Kinzer	Pitcher	1989
Walt Kinzie	Shortstop	1884
Mike Kircher	Pitcher	1920–1921
Bill Kissinger	Pitcher	1895–1897
Lou Klein	Second Base	1943, 1945, 1946, 1949
Nub Kleinke	Pitcher	1935, 1935, 1937
Ron Kline	Pitcher	1960
Steve Kline	Pitcher	2001–2004
Rudy Kling	Shortstop	1902

Billy Klusman	Second Base	1890
Clyde Kluttz	Catcher	1946
Alan Knicely	Catcher	1986
Jack Knight	Pitcher	1922
Mike Knode	Outfielder	1920
Ed Knouff	Pitcher	1887–1888
Darold Knowles	Pitcher	1979–1980
Will Koenigsmark	Pitcher	1919
Gary Kolb	Outfielder	1960, 1962–1963
Ed Konetchy	First Base	1907–1913
Jim Konstanty	Pitcher	1956
George Kopshaw	Catcher	1923
Ernie Koy	Outfielder	1940–1941
Lew Krausse	Pitcher	1973
Charlie Krehmeyer	Outfielder	1884
Kurt Krieger	Pitcher	1949, 1949, 1951
Howie Krist	Pitcher	1937–1938, 1941–1943, 1946
Rick Krivda	Pitcher	2000
Otto Krueger	Third Base	1900–1902
Ted Kubiak	Second Base	1971
Bill Kuehne	Third Base	1892
Ryan Kurosaki	Pitcher	1975
Whitey Kurowski	Third Base	1941–1949
Bob Kuzava	Pitcher	1957

L

Paul LaPalme	Pitcher	1955–1956
Mike Laga	First Base	1986–1988
Lerrin Lagrow	Pitcher	1976
Jeff Lahti	Pitcher	1982–1986
Eddie Lake	Shortstop	1939–1941
Steve Lake	Catcher	1986–1988
Dan Lally	Outfielder	1897
Jack Lamabe	Pitcher	1967
Fred Lamline	Pitcher	1915
Tom Lampkin	Catcher	1997–1998
Les Lancaster	Pitcher	1993
Hobie Landrith	Catcher	1957–1958
Don Landrum	Outfielder	1960–1962
Tito Landrum	Outfielder	1980–1987
Don Lang	Third Base	1948

Max Lanier	Pitcher	1938–1946,		Carlisle Littlejohn	Pitcher	1927–1928
		1949–1951		Danny Litwhiler	Outfielder	1943–1944,
Ray Lankford	Outfielder	1990–2001, 2004				1946
Dave Lapoint	Pitcher	1981–1984, 1987		Paddy Livingston	Catcher	1917
Ralph Lapointe	Shortstop	1948		Scott Livingstone	Third Base	1997
Bob Larmore	Shortstop	1918		Bobby Locke	Pitcher	1962
Lyn Lary	Shortstop	1939		Whitey Lockman	First Base	1956
Don Lassetter	Outfielder	1957		Tom Loftus	Outfielder	1883
Arlie Latham	Third Base	1883–1889, 1896		Bill Lohrman	Pitcher	1942
Mike Lavalliere	Catcher	1985–1986		Jeoff Long	Outfielder	1963–1964
Doc Lavan	Shortstop	1919–1924		Tom Long	Outfielder	1915–1917
Johnny Lavin	Outfielder	1884		Braden Looper	Pitcher	1998
Tom Lawless	Second Base	1985–1988		Art Lopatka	Pitcher	1945
Brooks Lawrence	Pitcher	1954–1955		Aurelio Lopez	Pitcher	1978
Scotty Layfield	Pitcher	2003		Joe Lotz	Pitcher	1916
Tom Leahy	Catcher	1905		Lynn Lovenguth	Pitcher	1957
Leron Lee	Outfielder	1969–1971		John Lovett	Pitcher	1903
Manuel Lee	Shortstop	1995		Grover Lowdermilk	Pitcher	1909, 1911
Jim Lentine	Outfielder	1978–1980		Lou Lowdermilk	Pitcher	1911–1912
(Unknown) Leonard	Outfielder	1892		Sean Lowe	Pitcher	1997–1998
Barry Lersch	Pitcher	1974		Peanuts Lowrey	Outfielder	1950–1954
Roy Leslie	First Base	1919		Con Lucid	Pitcher	1897
Dan Lewandowski	Pitcher	1951		Eric Ludwick	Pitcher	1996–1997
Bill Lewis	Catcher	1933		Bill Ludwig	Catcher	1908
Fred Lewis	Outfielder	1883–1884		Larry Luebbers	Pitcher	1999
Johnny Lewis	Outfielder	1964		Hector Luna	Second Base	2004–2005
Sixto Lezcano	Outfielder	1981				(Present)
Don Liddle	Pitcher	1956		Memo Luna	Pitcher	1954
Gene Lillard	Pitcher	1940		Ernie Lush	Outfielder	1910
Bob Lillis	Shortstop	1961		Johnny Lush	Pitcher	1907–1910
Mike Lincoln	Pitcher	2004 (Present)		Bill Lyons	Second Base	1983–1984
Johnny Lindell	Outfielder	1950		Denny Lyons	Third Base	1891, 1895
Jim Lindeman	Outfielder	1986–1989		George Lyons	Pitcher	1920
Jim Lindsey	Pitcher	1929–1934		Harry Lyons	Outfielder	1887–1888
Royce Lint	Pitcher	1954		Hersh Lyons	Pitcher	1941
Larry Lintz	Second Base	1975				
Frank Linzy	Pitcher	1970–1971		**M**		
Mark Littell	Pitcher	1978–1982		Bob Mabe	Pitcher	1958
Jeff Little	Pitcher	1980		John Mabry	Outfielder	1994–1998, 2001,
Mark Little	Left Field	1998				2004–2005 (Present)
Dick Littlefield	Pitcher	1956		Ken Mackenzie	Pitcher	1963
John Littlefield	Pitcher	1980		John Mackinson	Pitcher	1955

Name	Position	Years
Lonnie Maclin	Outfielder	1993
Max Macon	Pitcher	1938
Bill Magee	Pitcher	1901
Lee Magee	Outfielder	1911–1914
Sal Maglie	Pitcher	1958
Joe Magrane	Pitcher	1987–1990, 1992–1993
Art Mahaffey	Pitcher	1966
Mike Mahoney	Catcher	2005 (Present)
Mike Mahoney	First Base	1898
Duster Mails	Pitcher	1925–1926
Jim Mallory	Outfielder	1945
Gus Mancuso	Catcher	1928, 1930–1932, 1941–1942
Les Mann	Outfielder	1921–1923
Fred Manrique	Second Base	1986
Tom Mansell	Outfielder	1883
Rabbit Maranville	Shortstop	1927–1928
Walt Marbet	Pitcher	1913
Marty Marion	Shortstop	1940–1950
Roger Maris	Outfielder	1967–1968
Diegomar Markwell	Pitcher	2003–2004
Fred Marolewski	First Base	1953
Jason Marquis	Pitcher	2004–2005 (Present)
Eli Marrero	Catcher	1997–2003
Charlie Marshall	Catcher	1941
Doc Marshall	Catcher	1906–1908
Joe Marshall	Outfielder	1906
Fred Martin	Pitcher	1946, 1949–1950
John Martin	Pitcher	1980–1983
Morrie Martin	Pitcher	1957–1958
Pepper Martin	Outfielder	1928, 1930–1940,
Stu Martin	Second Base	1936–1940, 1944
Marty Martinez	Shortstop	1972
Silvio Martinez	Pitcher	1978–1981
Ted Martinez	Shortstop	1975
Tino Martinez	First Base	2002–2003
Ernie Mason	Pitcher	1894
Juan Mateo	Pitcher	2005 (Present)
Mike Matheny	Catcher	2000–2004
Greg Mathews	Pitcher	1986–1988, 1990
Mike Matthews	Pitcher	2000–2002
T. J. Mathews	Pitcher	1995–1997, 2001
Wally Mattick	Outfielder	1918
Gene Mauch	Second Base	1952
Harry Maupin	Pitcher	1898
Dal Maxvill	Shortstop	1962–1972
Jakie May	Pitcher	1917–1921
Jack McAdams	Pitcher	1911
Ike McAuley	Shortstop	1917
Bake McBride	Outfielder	1973–1977
George McBride	Shortstop	1905–1906
Pete McBride	Pitcher	1899
Harry McCaffery	Outfielder	1882–1883
Joe McCarthy	Catcher	1906
Tommy McCarthy	Outfielder	1888–1891
Lew McCarty	Catcher	1920–1921
Tim McCarver	Catcher	1959–1961, 1963–1969, 1973–1974
Jim McCauley	Catcher	1884
Pat McCauley	Catcher	1893
Bob McClure	Pitcher	1991–1992
Billy McCool	Pitcher	1970
Jim McCormick	Second Base	1892
Harry McCurdy	Catcher	1922–1923
Lindy McDaniel	Pitcher	1955–1962
Von McDaniel	Pitcher	1957–1958
Mickey McDermott	Pitcher	1961
Mike McDermott	Pitcher	1897
Keith McDonald	Catcher	2000–2001
Dewey McDougal	Pitcher	1895–1896
Sandy McDougal	Pitcher	1905
Will McEnaney	Pitcher	1979
Joe McEwing	Third Base	1998–1999
Guy McFadden	First Base	1895
Chappie McFarland	Pitcher	1902–1906
Ed McFarland	Catcher	1896–1897
Dan McGann	First Base	1900–1901
Chippy McGarr	Third Base	1888
Bill McGee	Pitcher	1935–1941
Willie McGee	Outfielder	1982–1990, 1996–1999

Dan McGeehan	Second Base	1911	Larry Miggins	Outfielder	1948, 1952
Willie McGill	Pitcher	1891	Pete Mikkelsen	Pitcher	1968
Jim McGinley	Pitcher	1904–1905	Eddie Miksis	Second Base	1957
Jumbo McGinnis	Pitcher	1882–1886	Aaron Miles	Second Base	2005 (Present)
Lynn McGlothen	Pitcher	1974–1976	Frank Millard	Second Base	1890
Stoney McGlynn	Pitcher	1906–1908	Bob Miller	Pitcher	1957, 1959–1961
Bob McGraw	Pitcher	1927	Chuck Miller	Outfielder	1913–1914
John McGraw	Third Base	1900	Doggie Miller	Catcher	1894–1895
Tom McGraw	Pitcher	1997	Dots Miller	First Base	1914–1917, 1919
Terry McGriff	Catcher	1994	Dusty Miller	Outfielder	1890, 1899
Mark McGrillis	Third Base	1892	Eddie Miller	Shortstop	1950
Mark McGwire	First Base	1997–2001	Elmer Miller	Outfielder	1912
Austin McHenry	Outfielder	1918–1922	Kohly Miller	Second Base	1892
Otto McIvor	Outfielder	1911	Stu Miller	Pitcher	1952–1954, 1956
Cody McKay	Catcher	2004	Jocko Milligan	Catcher	1888–1889
Ed McKean	Shortstop	1899	Buster Mills	Outfielder	1934
Ralph McLaurin	Outfielder	1908	Larry Milton	Pitcher	1903
Larry McLean	Catcher	1904, 1913	Minnie Minoso	Outfielder	1962
Jerry McNertney	Catcher	1971–1972	Bobby Mitchell	Pitcher	1882
Mart McQuaid	Second Base	1891	Clarence Mitchell	Pitcher	1928–1930
Brian McRae	Outfielder	2000	Johnny Mize	First Base	1936–1941
Trick McSorley	First Base	1886	Vinegar Bend Mizell	Pitcher	1952–1953,
Paul McSweeney	Second Base	1891			1956–1960
Larry McWilliams	Pitcher	1988	Herb Moford	Pitcher	1955
Lee Meadows	Pitcher	1915–1919	Mike Mohler	Pitcher	1999–2000
Joe Medwick	Outfielder	1932–1940,	Gabe Molina	Pitcher	2002–2003
		1947–1948	Yadier Molina	Catcher	2004–2005
Dad Meek	Catcher	1889–1890			(Present)
Miguel Mejia	Outfielder	1996	Fritz Mollwitz	First Base	1919
Roberto Mejia	Second Base	1997	Wally Moon	Outfielder	1954–1958
Sam Mejias	Outfielder	1976	Jim Mooney	Pitcher	1933–1934
Luis Melendez	Outfielder	1970–1976	Donnie Moore	Pitcher	1980
Steve Melter	Pitcher	1909	Gene Moore	Outfielder	1933–1935
Ted Menze	Outfielder	1918	Randy Moore	Outfielder	1937
John Mercer	First Base	1912	Terry Moore	Outfielder	1935–1942,
Kent Mercker	Pitcher	1998–1999			1946–1948
Lloyd Merritt	Pitcher	1957	Tommy Moore	Pitcher	1975
Sam Mertes	Outfielder	1906	Whitey Moore	Pitcher	1942
Steve Mesner	Third Base	1941	Jerry Morales	Outfielder	1978
Butch Metzger	Pitcher	1977	Bill Moran	Catcher	1892
Ed Mickelson	First Base	1950	Charlie Moran	Catcher	1903, 1908
Ed Mierkowicz	Outfielder	1950	Forrest More	Pitcher	1909

Bobby Morgan	Second Base	1956		Bert Myers	Third Base	1896
Eddie Morgan	Outfielder	1936		Hy Myers	Outfielder	1923–1925
Joe Morgan	Third Base	1964		Lynn Myers	Shortstop	1938–1939
Mike Morgan	Pitcher	1995–1996				
Gene Moriarity	Outfielder	1892		**N**		
John Morris	Outfielder	1986–1990		Mike Nagy	Pitcher	1973
Matt Morris	Pitcher	1997–1998, 2000–2005 (Present)		Sam Nahem	Pitcher	1941
				Sam Narron	Catcher	1935, 1942–1943
				Chris Narveson	Pitcher	2005 (Present)
Walter Morris	Shortstop	1908		Ken Nash	Shortstop	1914
Hap Morse	Shortstop	1911		Mike Naymick	Pitcher	1944
Charlie Morton	Outfielder	1882		Joe Neale	Pitcher	1890–1891
Walt Moryn	Outfielder	1960–1961		Mel Nelson	Pitcher	1960, 1968–1969
Jason Motte	Catcher	2005		Rocky Nelson	First Base	1949–1951, 1956
Mike Mowrey	Third Base	1909–1913		Art Nichols	Catcher	1901–1903
Jamie Moyer	Pitcher	1991		Kid Nichols	Pitcher	1904–1905
Dan Moylan	Catcher	2005		George Nicol	Outfielder	1890
Heinie Mueller	Outfielder	1920–1926		Hugh Nicol	Outfielder	1883–1886
Billy Muffett	Pitcher	1957–1958		Charlie Niebergall	Catcher	1921, 1923–1924
Mark Mulder	Pitcher	2005 (Present)		Tom Niedenfuer	Pitcher	1990
Tony Mullane	Pitcher	1883		Dick Niehaus	Pitcher	1913–1915
Jerry Mumphrey	Outfielder	1974–1979		Bert Niehoff	Second Base	1918
Red Munger	Pitcher	1943–1944, 1946–1952		Bob Nieman	Outfielder	1960–1961
				Tom Nieto	Catcher	1984–1985
Les Munns	Pitcher	1936		Tom Niland	Outfielder	1896
John Munyan	Catcher	1890–1891		Ramon Nivar	Outfielder	2005
Steve Mura	Pitcher	1982		Pete Noonan	Catcher	1906–1907
Simmy Murch	Second Base	1904–1905		Irv Noren	Outfielder	1957–1959
Tim Murchison	Pitcher	1917		Fred Norman	Pitcher	1970–1971
Wilbur Murdoch	Outfielder	1908		Lou North	Pitcher	1917, 1920–1924
Ed Murphy	Pitcher	1901–1903		Ron Northey	Outfielder	1947–1949
Howard Murphy	Outfielder	1909		Joe Nossek	Outfielder	1969–1970
Joe Murphy	Pitcher	1886–1887		Abraham Nunez	Second Base	2005 (Present)
John Murphy	Shortstop	1902		Howie Nunn	Pitcher	1959
Mike Murphy	Catcher	1912		Rich Nye	Pitcher	1970
Morgan Murphy	Catcher	1896–1897				
Rob Murphy	Pitcher	1993–1994		**O**		
Tom Murphy	Pitcher	1973		Dan O'Brien	Pitcher	1978–1979
Glenn Murray	Outfielder	2000		Johnny O'Brien	Second Base	1958
Red Murray	Outfielder	1906–1908		Jack O'Connor	Catcher	1899–1900
Stan Musial	Outfielder	1941–1944, 1946–1963		Paddy O'Connor	Catcher	1914
				Ken O'Dea	Catcher	1942–1946

Bob O'Farrell	Catcher	1925–1928, 1933, 1935
Bill O'Hara	Outfielder	1910
Tom O'Hara	Outfielder	1906–1907
Charley O'Leary	Shortstop	1913
Randy O'Neal	Pitcher	1987–1988
Denny O'Neil	First Base	1893
Jack O'Neill	Catcher	1902–1903
Mike O'Neill	Pitcher	1901–1904
Tip O'Neill	Outfielder	1884–1889, 1891
Charlie O'Rourke	—	1959
Patsy O'Rourke	Shortstop	1908
Tim O'Rourke	Third Base	1894
Rebel Oakes	Outfielder	1910–1913
Henry Oberbeck	Outfielder	1883
Ken Oberkfell	Third Base	1977–1984
Alex Ochoa	Outfielder	2003
Bruce Ogrodowski	Catcher	1936–1937
Kevin Ohme	Pitcher	2003
Jose Oliva	Third Base	1995
Ed Olivares	Outfielder	1960–1961
Omar Olivares	Pitcher	1990–1994
Darren Oliver	Pitcher	1998–1999
Gene Oliver	Catcher	1959, 1961–1963
Diomedes Olivo	Pitcher	1963
Al Olmsted	Pitcher	1980
Kevin Ool	Pitcher	2005
Jose Oquendo	Second Base	1986–1995
Luis Ordaz	Second Base	1997–1999
Joe Orengo	Third Base	1939–1940
Jesse Orosco	Pitcher	2000
Ernie Orsatti	Outfielder	1927–1935
William Ortega	Left Field	2001
Luis Ortiz	Third Base	2004
Donovan Osborne	Pitcher	1992–1993, 1995–1999
Champ Osteen	Shortstop	1908–1909
Claude Osteen	Pitcher	1974
Jim Otten	Pitcher	1980–1981
Joe Otten	Catcher	1895
Mickey Owen	Catcher	1937–1940
Rick Ownbey	Pitcher	1984, 1984, 1986

P

Ed Pabst	Outfielder	1890
Gene Packard	Pitcher	1917–1918
Dick Padden	Second Base	1901
Don Padgett	Catcher	1937–1941
Matt Pagnozzi	Catcher	2004
Tom Pagnozzi	Catcher	1987–1998
Phil Paine	Pitcher	1958
Lance Painter	Pitcher	1997–1999, 2003
Vicente Palacios	Pitcher	1994–1995
Orlando Palmeiro	Outfielder	2003
Lowell Palmer	Pitcher	1972
Al Papai	Pitcher	1948, 1950
Stan Papi	Third Base	1974
Erik Pappas	Catcher	1993–1994
Craig Paquette	Third Base	1999–2001
Freddy Parent	Shortstop	1899
Kelly Paris	Third Base	1982
Harry Parker	Pitcher	1970–1971, 1975
Roy Parker	Pitcher	1919
Roy Parmelee	Pitcher	1936
Chad Paronto	Pitcher	2003–2004
Jeff Parrett	Pitcher	1995–1996
Rhett Parrott	Pitcher	2004–2005 (Present)
Tom Parrott	Outfielder	1896
Stan Partenheimer	Pitcher	1945
Mike Pasquella	First Base	1919
Daryl Patterson	Pitcher	1971
Harry Patton	Pitcher	1910
Gene Paulette	First Base	1917–1919
Gil Paulsen	Pitcher	1925
George Paynter	Outfielder	1894
George Pearce	Pitcher	1917
Josh Pearce	Pitcher	2002–2004
Frank Pears	Pitcher	1893
Alex Pearson	Pitcher	1902
Jason Pearson	Pitcher	2003
Homer Peel	Outfielder	1927, 1930
Charlie Peete	Outfielder	1956
Heinie Peitz	Catcher	1892–1895, 1913

Name	Position	Years	Name	Position	Years
Joe Peitz	Outfielder	1894	Ted Power	Pitcher	1989
Geronimo Pena	Second Base	1990–1995	Joe Presko	Pitcher	1951–1954
Orlando Pena	Pitcher	1973–1974	Mike Proly	Pitcher	1976
Tony Pena	Catcher	1987–1989	George Puccinelli	Outfielder	1930, 1932
Terry Pendleton	Third Base	1984–1990	Albert Pujols	First Base	2001–2005
Ray Pepper	Outfielder	1932–1933			(Present)
Hub Perdue	Pitcher	1914–1915	Bill Pulsipher	Pitcher	2005
Eduardo Perez	First Base	1999–2000,	Bob Purkey	Pitcher	1965
		2002–2003	Ambrose Puttmann	Pitcher	1906
Mike Perez	Pitcher	1990–1994			
Pol Perritt	Pitcher	1912–1914	**Q**		
Gerald Perry	First Base	1991–1995	Joe Quest	Second Base	1883–1884
Pat Perry	Pitcher	1985–1987	Finners Quinlan	Outfielder	1913
Bill Pertica	Pitcher	1921–1923	Joe Quinn	Second Base	1893–1896,
Steve Peters	Pitcher	1987–1988			1898, 1900
Mark Petkovsek	Pitcher	1995–1998	Mark Quinn	Outfielder	2004
Jeff Pfeffer	Pitcher	1921–1924	Jamie Quirk	Catcher	1983
Ed Phelps	Catcher	1909–1910	Dan Quisenberry	Pitcher	1988–1989
Eddie Phillips	—	1953			
Mike Phillips	Shortstop	1977–1980	**R**		
Bill Phyle	Pitcher	1906	Roy Radebaugh	Pitcher	1911
Ron Piche	Pitcher	1966	Dave Rader	Catcher	1977
Charlie Pickett	Pitcher	1910	Scott Radinsky	Pitcher	1999–2000
George Pinkney	Third Base	1892	Ken Raffensberger	Pitcher	1939
Vada Pinson	Outfielder	1969	Brady Raggio	Pitcher	1997–1998
Cotton Pippen	Pitcher	1936	Gary Rajsich	First Base	1984
Phil Plantier	Outfielder	1997	John Raleigh	Pitcher	1909–1910
Tim Plodinec	Pitcher	1972	Milt Ramirez	Shortstop	1970–1971
Jamie Pogue	—	2001–2002	Mike Ramsey	Second Base	1978, 1980–1984
Tom Poholsky	Pitcher	1950–1951,	Toad Ramsey	Pitcher	1889–1890
		1954–1956	Dick Rand	Catcher	1953, 1955
Placido Polanco	Second Base	1998–2002	Vic Raschi	Pitcher	1954–1955
Cliff Politte	Pitcher	1998	Eric Rasmussen	Pitcher	1975–1978,
Howie Pollet	Pitcher	1941–1943,			1982–1983
		1946–1951	Tommy Raub	Catcher	1906
Bill Popp	Pitcher	1902	Floyd Rayford	Third Base	1983
Colin Porter	Center Field	2004	Bugs Raymond	Pitcher	1907–1908
Darrell Porter	Catcher	1981–1985	Britt Reames	Pitcher	2000
Jay Porter	Catcher	1959	Art Rebel	Outfielder	1945
Mike Potter	Outfielder	1976–1977	Phil Redding	Pitcher	1912–1913
Nels Potter	Pitcher	1936	Prentice Redman	Outfielder	2005
Jack Powell	Pitcher	1899–1901	Milt Reed	Shortstop	1911

Name	Position	Years
Ron Reed	Pitcher	1975
Bill Reeder	Pitcher	1949
Jimmie Reese	Second Base	1932
Tom Reilly	Shortstop	1908–1909
Art Reinhart	Pitcher	1919, 1925–1928
Jack Reis	Pitcher	1911
Ken Reitz	Third Base	1972–1975, 1977–1980
Edgar Renteria	Shortstop	1999–2004
Bob Repass	Second Base	1939
Rip Repulski	Outfielder	1953–1956
George Rettger	Pitcher	1891
Jerry Reuss	Pitcher	1969–1971
Al Reyes	Pitcher	2004–2005 (Present)
Anthony Reyes	Pitcher	2005 (Present)
Bob Reynolds	Pitcher	1971
Ken Reynolds	Pitcher	1975
Flint Rhem	Pitcher	1924–1928, 1930–1932, 1934, 1936
Bob Rhoads	Pitcher	1903
Charlie Rhodes	Pitcher	1906, 1908–1909
Dennis Ribant	Pitcher	1969
Del Rice	Catcher	1945–1955, 1960
Hal Rice	Outfielder	1948–1953
Chris Richard	First Base	2000
Lee Richard	Shortstop	1976
Bill Richardson	First Base	1901
Gordie Richardson	Pitcher	1964
Pete Richert	Pitcher	1974
Don Richmond	Third Base	1951
Dave Ricketts	Catcher	1963, 1965, 1967–1969
Dick Ricketts	Pitcher	1959
John Ricks	Third Base	1891, 1894
Elmer Rieger	Pitcher	1910
Joe Riggert	Outfielder	1914
Lew Riggs	Third Base	1934
Andy Rincon	Pitcher	1980–1982
Jimmy Ring	Pitcher	1927
Tink Riviere	Pitcher	1921
Skipper Roberts	Catcher	1913
Hank Robinson	Pitcher	1914–1915
Kerry Robinson	Outfielder	2001–2003
Wilbert Robinson	Catcher	1900
Yank Robinson	Second Base	1885–1889, 1891
Jack Roche	Catcher	1914–1915, 1917
Joe Rodriguez	Pitcher	2000, 2000, 2002
John Rodriguez	Outfielder	2005 (Present)
Nerio Rodriguez	Pitcher	2002
Rich Rodriguez	Pitcher	1994–1995
Preacher Roe	Pitcher	1938
Wally Roettger	Outfielder	1927–1929, 1931
Cookie Rojas	Second Base	1970
Stan Rojek	Shortstop	1951
Scott Rolen	Third Base	2002–2005 (Present)
Ray Rolling	Second Base	1912
Johnny Romano	Catcher	1967
John Romonosky	Pitcher	1953
Marc Ronan	Catcher	1993
Gene Roof	Outfielder	1981–1983
Jorge Roque	Outfielder	1970–1972
Chief Roseman	Outfielder	1890
Jack Rothrock	Outfielder	1934–1935
Stan Royer	Third Base	1991–1994
Dave Rucker	Pitcher	1983–1984
Ken Rudolph	Catcher	1975–1976
Jack Russell	Pitcher	1940
Paul Russell	Second Base	1894
Evan Rust	Pitcher	2005 (Present)
Brendan Ryan	Shortstop	2005 (Present)
Jack Ryan	Catcher	1901–1903
Mike Ryan	Third Base	1895
Mike Ryba	Pitcher	1935–1938

S

Name	Position	Years
Chris Sabo	Third Base	1995
Ray Sadecki	Pitcher	1960–1966, 1975
Bob Sadowski	Third Base	1960
Mark Salas	Catcher	1984
Slim Sallee	Pitcher	1908–1916
Ike Samuls	Third Base	1895

Name	Position	Years	Name	Position	Years
Orlando Sanchez	Catcher	1981–1983	George Scott	Pitcher	1920
Ray Sanders	First Base	1942–1945	Tony Scott	Outfielder	1977–1981
Reggie Sanders	Outfielder	2004–2005 (Present)	Scott Seabol	Third Base	2005 (Present)
			Kim Seaman	Pitcher	1979–1980
War Sanders	Pitcher	1903–1904	Shawn Sedlacek	Pitcher	2005
Rafael Santana	Shortstop	1983	Diego Segui	Pitcher	1972–1973
Al Santorini	Pitcher	1971–1973	Epp Sell	Pitcher	1922–1923
Bill Sarni	Catcher	1951–1952, 1954–1956	Carey Selph	Third Base	1929
			Walter Sessi	Outfielder	1941, 1946
Luis Saturria	Outfielder	2000–2001	George Seward	Outfielder	1882
Ed Sauer	Outfielder	1949	Jimmy Sexton	Shortstop	1983
Hank Sauer	Outfielder	1956	Mike Shannon	Third Base	1962–1970
Ted Savage	Outfielder	1965–1967	Spike Shannon	Outfielder	1904–1906
Carl Sawatski	Catcher	1960–1963	Wally Shannon	Second Base	1959–1960
Steve Scarsone	Second Base	1997	Bobby Shantz	Pitcher	1962–1964
Jimmie Schaffer	Catcher	1961–1962	Al Shaw	Outfielder	1907–1909
Bobby Schang	Catcher	1927	Don Shaw	Pitcher	1971–1972
John Schappert	Pitcher	1882	Danny Shay	Shortstop	1904–1905
Bob Scheffing	Catcher	1951	Gerry Shea	Catcher	1905
Carl Scheib	Pitcher	1954	Danny Sheaffer	Catcher	1995–1997
Richie Scheinblum	Outfielder	1974	Jimmy Sheckard	Outfielder	1913
Bill Schindler	Catcher	1920	Biff Sheehan	Outfielder	1895–1896
Freddy Schmidt	Pitcher	1944, 1946–1947	Ray Shepardson	Catcher	1924
Walter Schmidt	Catcher	1925	Bill Sherdel	Pitcher	1918–1930, 1932
Willard Schmidt	Pitcher	1952–1953, 1955–1957	Kevin Sheredy	—	1996–2002
			Tim Sherrill	Pitcher	1990–1991
Red Schoendienst	Second Base	1945–1956, 1961–1963	Charlie Shields	Pitcher	1907
			Vince Shields	Pitcher	1924
Dick Schofield	Shortstop	1953–1958, 1968, 1968, 1971	Ralph Shinners	Outfielder	1925
			Bob Shirley	Pitcher	1981
Ossee Schreckengost	Catcher	1899	Burt Shotton	Outfielder	1919–1923
Pop Schriver	Catcher	1901	Clyde Shoun	Pitcher	1938–1942
Heinie Schuble	Shortstop	1927, 1927, 1936	John Shoupe	Shortstop	1882
Johnny Schulte	Catcher	1927	Frank Shugart	Shortstop	1893–1894
Barney Schultz	Pitcher	1955, 1963–1965	Dick Siebert	First Base	1937–1938
Buddy Schultz	Pitcher	1977–1979	Sonny Siebert	Pitcher	1974
Joe Schultz	Outfielder	1919–1924	Curt Simmons	Pitcher	1960–1966
John Schultz	Catcher	1891	Ted Simmons	Catcher	1968–1980
Walt Schulz	Pitcher	1920	Jason Simontacchi	Pitcher	2002–2004
Skip Schumaker	Center Field	2005 (Present)	Dick Simpson	Outfielder	1968
Ferdie Schupp	Pitcher	1919–1921	Dick Sisler	First Base	1946–1947, 1952–1953
Lou Scoffic	Outfielder	1936			

Name	Position	Years
Ted Sizemore	Second Base	1971–1975
Bob Skinner	Outfielder	1964–1966
Gordon Slade	Shortstop	1933
Jack Slattery	Catcher	1906
Enos Slaughter	Outfielder	1938–1942, 1946–1953
Heathcliff Slocumb	Pitcher	1999–2000
Bill Smiley	Second Base	1882
Bill Smith	Pitcher	1958–1959
Bob Smith	Pitcher	1957
Bobby Gene Smith	Outfielder	1957–1959, 1962
Bryn Smith	Pitcher	1990–1992
Bud Smith	Pitcher	2001–2002
Charley Smith	Third Base	1966
Earl Smith	Catcher	1928–1930
Frank Smith	Pitcher	1955
Fred Smith	Third Base	1917
Germany Smith	Shortstop	1898
Hal Smith	Catcher	1956–1961
Jack Smith	Outfielder	1915–1926
Jud Smith	Third Base	1893
Keith Smith	Outfielder	1979–1980
Lee Smith	Pitcher	1990–1993
Lonnie Smith	Outfielder	1982–1985
Ozzie Smith	Shortstop	1982–1996
Reggie Smith	Outfielder	1974–1976
Tom Smith	Pitcher	1898
Travis Smith	Pitcher	2002
Wally Smith	Third Base	1911–1912
Willie Smith	Pitcher	1994
Homer Smoot	Outfielder	1902–1906
Red Smyth	Outfielder	1917–1918
Frank Snyder	Catcher	1912–1919, 1927
Clint Sodowsky	Pitcher	1999
Ray Soff	Pitcher	1986–1987
Eddie Solomon	Pitcher	1976
Lary Sorensen	Pitcher	1981
Elias Sosa	Pitcher	1975
Allen Sothoron	Pitcher	1924–1926
Billy Southworth	Outfielder	1926–1927, 1929
Chris Speier	Shortstop	1984
Daryl Spencer	Shortstop	1960–1961
Ed Spiezio	Third Base	1964–1968
Scipio Spinks	Pitcher	1972–1973
Paul Spoljaric	Pitcher	1999–2000
Ed Sprague	Pitcher	1973
Jack Spring	Pitcher	1964
Russ Springer	Pitcher	2003
Joe Sprinz	Catcher	1933
Tuck Stainback	Outfielder	1938
Gerry Staley	Pitcher	1947–1954
Harry Staley	Pitcher	1895
Tracy Stallard	Pitcher	1965–1966
Virgil Stallcup	Shortstop	1952–1953
Pete Standridge	Pitcher	1911
Eddie Stanky	Second Base	1952–1953
Harry Stanton	Catcher	1900
Ray Starr	Pitcher	1932
Gene Stechschulte	Pitcher	2000–2002
Bill Steele	Pitcher	1910–1914
Bob Steele	Pitcher	1916–1917
Bill Stein	Third Base	1972–1973
Jake Stenzel	Outfielder	1898–1899
Ray Stephens	Catcher	1990–1991
Bob Stephenson	Shortstop	1955
Garrett Stephenson	Pitcher	1999–2000, 2002–2003
Stuffy Stewart	Second Base	1916–1917
Bob Stinson	Catcher	1971
Jack Stivetts	Pitcher	1889–1891
Chuck Stobbs	Pitcher	1958
Milt Stock	Third Base	1919–1923
Dean Stone	Pitcher	1959
Tige Stone	Outfielder	1923
Alan Storke	First Base	1909
Todd Stottlemyre	Pitcher	1996–1998
Allyn Stout	Pitcher	1931–1933
Gabby Street	Catcher	1931
Cub Stricker	Second Base	1892
George Strief	Second Base	1883–1884
Joe Stripp	Third Base	1938

Name	Position	Year	Name	Position	Year
Al Struve	Catcher	1884	Chuck Taylor	Pitcher	1969–1971
Johnny Stuart	Pitcher	1922–1925	Ed Taylor	Pitcher	1903
John Stuper	Pitcher	1982–1984	Jack Taylor	Pitcher	1898
Willie Sudhoff	Pitcher	1897–1901	Jack Taylor	Pitcher	1904–1906
Joe Sugden	Catcher	1898	Joe Taylor	Outfielder	1958
Dan Sullivan	Catcher	1885	Ron Taylor	Pitcher	1963–1965
Harry Sullivan	Pitcher	1909	Bud Teachout	Pitcher	1932
Joe Sullivan	Shortstop	1896	Patsy Tebeau	First Base	1899–1900
Sleeper Sullivan	Catcher	1882–1883	Garry Templeton	Shortstop	1976–1981
Suter Sullivan	Third Base	1898	Gene Tenace	Catcher	1981–1982
Kid Summers	Catcher	1893	Greg Terlecky	Pitcher	1975
Tom Sunkel	Pitcher	1937, 1937, 1939	Scott Terry	Pitcher	1987–1991
			Dick Terwilliger	Pitcher	1932
Jeff Suppan	Pitcher	2004–2005 (Present)	Bob Tewksbury	Pitcher	1989–1994
			Moe Thacker	Catcher	1963
Max Surkont	Pitcher	1956	Tommy Thevenow	Shortstop	1924–1928
Rick Sutcliffe	Pitcher	1994	Jake Thielman	Pitcher	1905–1906
Gary Sutherland	Second Base	1978	Roy Thomas	Pitcher	1978–1980
Bruce Sutter	Pitcher	1981–1984	Tom Thomas	Pitcher	1899–1900
Jack Sutthoff	Pitcher	1899	Brad Thompson	Pitcher	2005 (Present)
John Sutton	Pitcher	1977			
Larry Sutton	Outfielder	2000–2001	Gus Thompson	Pitcher	1906
Mark Sweeney	Outfielder	1995–1997	Mark Thompson	Pitcher	1999–2000
Pete Sweeney	Third Base	1889–1890	Mike Thompson	Pitcher	1973–1974
Charlie Swindells	Catcher	1904	Milt Thompson	Outfielder	1989–1992
Steve Swisher	Catcher	1978–1980	John Thornton	Pitcher	1892
Bob Sykes	Pitcher	1979–1981	Bobby Tiefenauer	Pitcher	1952, 1955, 1961
Lou Sylvester	Outfielder	1887	Mike Timlin	Pitcher	2000–2002
			Bud Tinning	Pitcher	1935
T			Bobby Tolan	Outfielder	1965–1968
Jeff Tabaka	Pitcher	2001	Brett Tomko	Pitcher	2003
So Taguchi	Outfielder	2002–2005 (Present)	Fred Toney	Pitcher	1923
			Specs Toporcer	Shortstop	1921–1928
John Tamargo	Catcher	1976–1978	Joe Torre	Catcher	1969–1974
Dennis Tankersley	Pitcher	2005	Mike Torrez	Pitcher	1967–1971
Lee Tate	Shortstop	1958–1959	Paul Toth	Pitcher	1962
Fernando Tatis	Third Base	1998–2000	Harry Trekell	Pitcher	1913
Don Taussig	Outfielder	1961	Coaker Triplett	Outfielder	1941–1943
Julian Tavarez	Pitcher	2004–2005 (Present)	Mike Trost	Catcher	1890
			Bill Trotter	Pitcher	1944
Carl Taylor	Catcher	1970	Tommy Tucker	First Base	1898

John Tudor	Pitcher	1985–1988, 1990		David Wainhouse	Pitcher	2000
Oscar Tuero	Pitcher	1918–1920		Adam Wainwright	Pitcher	2005 (Present)
Lee Tunnell	Pitcher	1987		Bill Walker	Pitcher	1933–1936
Tuck Turner	Outfielder	1896–1898		Duane Walker	Outfielder	1988
Art Twineham	Catcher	1893–1894		Harry Walker	Outfielder	1940–1943, 1946,
Mike Tyson	Second Base	1972–1979				1950, 1951, 1955
				Larry Walker	Outfielder	2004–2005
U						(Present)
Bob Uecker	Catcher	1964–1965		Oscar Walker	Outfielder	1882
Tom Underwood	Pitcher	1977		Roy Walker	Pitcher	1921–1922
Jack Urban	Pitcher	1959		Speed Walker	First Base	1923
Tom Urbani	Pitcher	1993–1996		Tom Walker	Pitcher	1976
Jose Uribe	Shortstop	1984		Bobby Wallace	Shortstop	1899–1901,
John Urrea	Pitcher	1977–1980				1917–1918
Lon Ury	First Base	1903		Mike Wallace	Pitcher	1975–1976
				Ty Waller	Third Base	1980
V				Denny Walling	Third Base	1988–1990
Benny Valenzuela	Third Base	1958		Samuel Walton	Pitcher	2005
Fernando Valenzuela	Pitcher	1997		Dick Ward	Pitcher	1935
Jay Van Noy	Outfielder	1951		Cy Warmoth	Pitcher	1916
Andy Van Slyke	Outfielder	1983–1986		Lon Warneke	Pitcher	1937–1942
Dazzy Vance	Pitcher	1933–1934		John Warner	Catcher	1905
Bill Vandyke	Outfielder	1892		Bill Warwick	Catcher	1925–1926
John Vann	—	1913		Carl Warwick	Outfielder	1961–1962,
Emil Verban	Second Base	1944–1946				1964–1965
Dave Veres	Pitcher	2000–2002		Ray Washburn	Pitcher	1961–1969
Johnny Vergez	Third Base	1936		Gary Waslewski	Pitcher	1969
Ernie Vick	Catcher	1922, 1924–1926		B. J. Waszgis	Catcher	2001–2002
Hector Villanueva	Catcher	1993		Steve Waterbury	Pitcher	1976
Fernando Vina	Second Base	2000–2003		George Watkins	Outfielder	1930–1933
Bob Vines	Pitcher	1924		Allen Watson	Pitcher	1993–1995
Bill Virdon	Outfielder	1955–1956		Milt Watson	Pitcher	1916–1917
Joe Visner	Outfielder	1891		Art Weaver	Catcher	1902–1903
Dave Vonohlen	Pitcher	1983–1984		John Webb	Pitcher	2005
Bill Voss	Outfielder	1972		Skeeter Webb	Shortstop	1932
Brad Voyles	Pitcher	2005		Herm Wehmeier	Pitcher	1956–1958
Pete Vuckovich	Pitcher	1978–1980		Clint Weibl	Pitcher	1996–2002
				Bob Weiland	Pitcher	1937–1940
W				Curt Welch	Outfielder	1885–1887
Ben Wade	Pitcher	1954		Jake Wells	Catcher	1890
Leon Wagner	Outfielder	1960		Perry Werden	First Base	1892–1893

Bill Werle	Pitcher	1952
Wally Westlake	Outfielder	1951–1952
Gus Weyhing	Pitcher	1900
Dick Wheeler	Outfielder	1918
Harry Wheeler	Outfielder	1884
Jimmy Whelan	—	1913
Pete Whisenant	Outfielder	1955
Lew Whistler	First Base	1893
Abe White	Pitcher	1937
Bill White	Shortstop	1888
Bill White	First Base	1959–1965, 1969
Ernie White	Pitcher	1940–1943
Gabe White	Pitcher	2005
Hal White	Pitcher	1953–1954
Jerry White	Outfielder	1986
Rick White	Pitcher	2002
Burgess Whitehead	Second Base	1933–1935
Mark Whiten	Outfielder	1993–1994
Fred Whitfield	First Base	1962
Art Whitney	Third Base	1891
Bill Whitrock	Pitcher	1890
Possum Whitted	Outfielder	1912–1914
Bob Wicker	Pitcher	1901–1903
Floyd Wicker	Outfielder	1968
Chris Widger	Catcher	2003
Bill Wight	Pitcher	1958
Fred Wigington	Pitcher	1923
Del Wilber	Catcher	1946–1949
Hoyt Wilhelm	Pitcher	1957
Denney Wilie	Outfielder	1911–1912
Rick Wilkins	Catcher	2000
Ted Wilks	Pitcher	1944–1951
Jimy Williams	Shortstop	1966–1967
Otto Williams	Shortstop	1902–1903
Stan Williams	Pitcher	1971
Steamboat Williams	Pitcher	1914, 1916
Woody Williams	Pitcher	2001–2004
Howie Williamson	—	1928
Joe Willis	Pitcher	1911–1913
Ron Willis	Pitcher	1966–1969
Vic Willis	Pitcher	1910

Charlie Wilson	Shortstop	1932–1933, 1935
Chief Wilson	Outfielder	1914–1916
Craig Wilson	Third Base	1989–1992
Jimmie Wilson	Catcher	1928–1933
Zeke Wilson	Pitcher	1899
Jim Winford	Pitcher	1932, 1934–1937
Ivey Wingo	Catcher	1911–1914
Tom Winsett	Outfielder	1935
Rick Wise	Pitcher	1972–1973
Corky Withrow	Outfielder	1963
Bobby Witt	Pitcher	1998
Kevin Witt	—	2003–2004
Jimmy Wolf	Outfielder	1892
Harry Wolter	Outfielder	1907
Tony Womack	Shortstop	2004
John Wood	Pitcher	1896
Gene Woodburn	Pitcher	1911–1912
Hal Woodeshick	Pitcher	1965–1967
Tracy Woodson	Third Base	1992–1993
Frank Woodward	Pitcher	1919
Floyd Wooldridge	Pitcher	1955
Todd Worrell	Pitcher	1985–1989, 1992
Red Worthington	Outfielder	1934
Jamey Wright	Pitcher	2002
Mel Wright	Pitcher	1954–1955

Y

Esteban Yan	Pitcher	2003
Stan Yerkes	Pitcher	1901–1903
Ray Yochim	Pitcher	1948–1949
Babe Young	First Base	1948
Bobby Young	Second Base	1948
Cy Young	Pitcher	1899–1900
Dmitri Young	Outfielder	1996–1997
Gerald Young	Outfielder	1994
J. B. Young	Pitcher	1892
Pep Young	Second Base	1941, 1945
Joel Youngblood	Outfielder	1977
Eddie Yuhas	Pitcher	1952–1953
Sal Yvars	Catcher	1953–1954

				Todd Zeile	Third Base	1989–1995
Z				Bart Zeller	Catcher	1970
Chris Zachary	Pitcher	1971		Bill Zies	Catcher	1891
Elmer Zacher	Outfielder	1910		Eddie Zimmerman	Third Base	1906
George Zackert	Pitcher	1911–1912		Ed Zmich	Pitcher	1910–1911
Dave Zearfoss	Catcher	1904–1905				

DATE			